LIVING FREE
Elsa and her Cubs

First published 1961 by William Collins Sons and Co Ltd
14 St James's Place, London SW1
First published in this abridged edition in Lions 1972
Second Impression September 1972
Third Impression 1973
Fourth Impression 1975

© Joy Adamson, 1961

Printed in Great Britain
by Richard Clay (The Chaucer Press) Ltd
Bungay, Suffolk

CONTENTS

AUTHOR'S NOTE

Since Elsa's cubs were born I have kept notes in which I have recorded what we observed of Elsa and her family when we were in camp. *Living Free* is based on these notes and this explains its form, and the use of the present tense in relation to Elsa.

All the experiences recounted in this book were shared with my husband George, and it could not have been written without him. I would like to acknowledge my gratitude to everyone who, whether in an official or a private capacity, made it possible for us to spend so much time at Elsa's camp. I would also like to thank all those who helped me with *Born Free* and have helped again in the publication of *Living Free*.

1. ELSA MATES WITH
A WILD LION

It was between 29th August and 4th September 1959 that my husband George actually saw Elsa and her lion courting.

When on his return to Isiolo he told me what he had seen I could hardly bear not to start off for camp alone, for I was afraid that Elsa might now follow her mate into a world beyond our reach.

But when we arrived she was there waiting for us by the big rock close to the car track.

As our tents were being pitched her lion started calling and during the night he circled round the camp, while she remained with George eating heartily and quite uninterested in her mate's appeal. At dawn we heard the lion still calling but from much farther away.

For two days she remained in camp eating so enormously that she was too sleepy to move till the afternoon when she went out fishing with George.

During the third night she ate so much that we were quite worried about her; yet in the morning, in spite of her bulging belly, she trotted into the bush with us and first stalked two jackals and then a flock of guinea fowl. Of course, each time she closed in on them they flew off, whereupon she sat down and licked her paws.

On our walk home Elsa, full of high spirits and affection, rolled me over several times in the sand.

That night she slept in front of my tent, but just before dawn her lion started calling and she went off in his direction.

Their calls were easy to distinguish; Elsa has a very deep guttural voice, but after her initial roar only gives two or three whuffing grunts, whereas her lion's voice is less deep and after his roar he always gives at least ten or twelve grunts.

During Elsa's absence we broke camp and left for Isiolo

7

hoping that she was in the company of her mate.

We returned to the camp on 10th October.

It was three weeks since we had left Elsa; an hour after our arrival we saw her swimming across the river to greet us, but instead of the exuberant welcome she usually gave us, she walked slowly up to me. She did not seem to be hungry and was exceptionally gentle and quiet. Patting her, I noticed that her skin had become extremely soft and her coat unusually glossy. She was pregnant. There was no doubt about it. She must have conceived a month ago.

It is widely believed that a pregnant lioness who is handicapped in hunting by her condition, is helped by one or two other lionesses who act as 'aunts.' They are also supposed to assist in looking after the new-born cubs, for the male is not of much practical use on such occasions and, indeed, is often not allowed near the young lions for some weeks.

Since poor Elsa had no 'aunts,' it would be our job to replace them. George and I talked over plans to help to feed her and avoid any risk of her injuring herself.

I was to stay in camp as much as I could and, at the nearest Game Scout Post, some twenty-five miles away, we would establish a herd of goats from which I could collect a few in my truck at regular intervals.

Nuru would remain with me to help with Elsa and Makedde would guard us with his rifle, Ibrahim could drive and I would keep one boy, the Toto (the word Toto means child in Swahili), to act as personal servant.

George would visit us as often as his work allowed.

As though she had understood our conversation, Elsa hopped on to my camp bed as soon as it was made ready and looked as if she thought it the only suitable place for someone in her condition.

From now on she took possession of it, and when next morning, as I did not feel well, I had it carried down to the studio, she came to share it with me. This was uncomfortable, so after a time I tipped it over and rolled her off. This indignity caused her to retire, offended, into the river reeds till the late afternoon when it was time for our walk.

When I called her she stared at me intently, advanced determinedly up to my bed, stepped on to it, squatted, lifted her tail and did something she had never before done in so unsuitable a place. Then with a very self-satisfied expression she jumped down and took the lead on our walk.

Apparently, now that she had had her revenge everything was again all right between us.

I observed that her movements were very slow and that even the noise of elephants close by only made her cock her ears. That night she rested in George's tent, unresponsive to the call of a lion who seemed to be very near the camp.

As in the early morning the lion was still calling, we took Elsa for a walk in his direction. There, to our surprise, we found the spoor of two lions.

When she began to show an interest in these pug marks we left her and returned home. She did not come back that night. The next day Elsa again stayed away. Hoping to make the lions kindly disposed towards her, George shot a buck and left it as a farewell gift; then we returned to Isiolo.

After we had spent two weeks at home we decided that it was time to go and see Elsa. It was dark when we reached camp, but Elsa appeared within a few moments. She was extremely thin, very hungry and had deep, bleeding gashes and bites on her neck, and also the claw marks of a lion on her back.

While she gnawed at the meat we had brought and I dressed her wounds, she responded by licking me and rubbing her head against mine.

During the night we heard her dragging the carcase down to the river and splashing across with it, and later we heard her returning. Shortly afterwards some baboons gave an alarm and were answered by a lion across the river. Elsa replied from our side with soft moans. Very early in the morning she tried to force her way through the wicker door of the thorn enclosure which surrounds my tent. She pushed her head half-through but then got stuck. Her attempt to free herself caused the door to give way and she finally entered wearing the gate round her neck like a

9

collar. I freed her at once but she seemed restless and in need of reassurance, for she sucked my thumb frantically.

She was now rather heavy and all exercise had become an effort to her.

During the following days Elsa shared her time between her mate and me. On our last night in camp Elsa made a terrific meal of goat and then, very heavy in the belly, went to join her lion who had been calling for her for many hours. Her absence gave us an excellent opportunity to leave for Isiolo.

In the second week of November George sent a patrol of Game Scouts out to deal with poachers while he and I went again to the camp to look for Elsa.

For some hours we walked through the bush, calling to her and at intervals shooting into the air, but there was no response. After dark a lion began to call from the direction of the Big Rock, but we listened in vain for Elsa's voice.

We had run out of thunder flashes so when it became dark all we could do to let her know that we were there was to turn on the penetrating howl of the air-raid siren, a relic of Mau-Mau days. In the past it had often brought her into camp.

It was answered by the lion; we sounded it again and again he replied, and this strange conversation went on until it was interrupted by Elsa's arrival. She knocked us all over; as her body was wet we realised that she must have swum across the river and had come from the opposite direction to that from which the lion was calling.

She seemed very fit and was not hungry. She left at dawn but returned at tea-time when we were setting out for our walk. We climbed up the Big Rock and sat there watching the sun sink like a fire-ball behind the indigo hills.

At first Elsa blended into the warm reddish colour of the rock as if she were part of it, then she was silhouetted against the fading sky in which a full moon was rising. I imagined Elsa in the future playing with her happy little cubs on this rock, cubs whose father was a wild lion: and at this very moment he might be waiting nearby. She rolled on her back and hugged me close to her. Carefully I laid my hand below her ribs to feel whether any life were moving within her, but she pushed it away making me feel as though I had committed an indiscretion.

Soon we had to return to camp, to the safety of our thorn enclosure, and the lamps and rifles with which we armed ourselves against those dark hours in which Elsa's real life began.

This was the moment at which we parted, each to return to our own world.

Elsa kept away during that night and the following day. In the afternoon we went to look for her. As I came near to the rock, I called out to warn her of our approach but got no reply. It was only when we had climbed on to the saddle where we had sat on the previous evening that we suddenly heard an alarming growl, followed by crashes and the sound of wood breaking inside the big cleft below us. We rushed as fast as we could to the top of the nearest rock, then we heard Elsa's voice very close and saw her lion making away swiftly through the bush. Elsa looked up at us, paused and silently rushed after her mate.

We waited until it was nearly dark and then called Elsa again. To our surprise she came trotting out of the bush, returned to camp with us and spent the night there, going off only in the early morning.

The next evening was lit by lightning, a sure sign that the rains would start soon. The transformation which always results from the onset of the rains is something which cannot be imagined by anyone who has not actually witnessed it.

A few days before we had been surrounded by grey, dry, crackling bush, in which long white thorns provided the only variation in colour. Now, on every side there was lush tropical vegetation decked with myriads of multi-coloured flowers, and the air was heavy with their scent.

In camp, evening is the time that I like best, for it is then that one becomes aware of the monotonous vibrations of the crickets and the rumble of the elephants, the hum of the bush, pierced occasionally by the cry of some nocturnal animal.

It is then too that one sees the great belt of light, some ten feet wide, formed by thousands upon thousands of fireflies whose green phosphorescence bridges the shoulder-high grass.

I had spent may rainy seasons in camp but never before had I seen such a brilliant display.

George had gone back to Isiolo, and when he returned to camp he brought a zebra for Elsa. This was a special treat. As soon as she heard the vibrations of the car she appeared, spotted the 'kill' and tried to pull the carcase out of the Land-Rover. Then, finding it too heavy for her, she walked over to where the boys were standing and jerking her head at the zebra made it plain that she needed help. They hauled the heavy animal a short distance amid much laughter and then waited for Elsa to start her meal. To our astonishment, although zebra was her favourite meat she did not eat but stood by the river roaring in her loudest voice.

We presumed that she was inviting her mate to join in the feast. This would have been good lion manners, for according to the recorded habit of prides, while the females do most of the killing, they then have to wait to satisfy their hunger until the lion has had his fill.

The next morning she swam across the heavily flooded river, came up to the zebra and roared repeatedly in the direction of the rocky range which is on our side of the river.

I noticed that she had a deep gash across one of her front paws, but she refused to have it dressed, and after she had eaten as much as she could, she went off towards the rocks.

That night it rained for eight hours, and the river turned into a torrent which it would have been very dangerous for Elsa to cross even though she is a powerful swimmer. I was therefore very pleased to see her in the morning returning from the Big Rock.

Her knee was very swollen and she allowed me to attend to her cut paw.

For several days she divided her time between us and her lion.

When George returned from a patrol he brought Elsa a goat. Usually she dragged her 'kill' into his tent, presumably to avoid the trouble of having to guard it, but this time she left it lying beside the car in a spot which could not be seen from the tent. During the night her mate came and had a good feed; we wondered whether this was what she had intended.

Next evening we took the precaution of placing some meat at a certain distance from the camp, for we did not want to encourage him to come too close.

Soon after dark we heard him dragging it away and in the morning Elsa joined him.

We were now faced with a problem. We wanted to help Elsa, who was increasingly handicapped by her pregnancy, by providing her with regular food, but we did not wish to interfere with her relations with her mate by our continued presence in the camp. He had a good right to resent this, but did he in fact object to us? On the whole, we thought that he did not, and I think we were justified in our opinion for, during the next six months, though we did not see him, we often heard his characteristic ten or twelve whuffing grunts and recognised his spoor, which proved that he remained Elsa's constant companion.

Though he still kept out of our sight, he had become bolder and bolder, but an extraordinary kind of truce seemed to have been established between us. He had come to know our routine as intimately as we had come to know his habits. He shared Elsa's company with us and we thought that in return he could fairly expect an occasional meal as compensation.

In view of his attitude we stilled our qualms of conscience and stayed on.

On the 1st December, George, Elsa and I were walking in the bush. Suddenly I heard George give a whistle and looking up saw a herd of some twenty buffalo cows, many of them followed by calves, making their way to the water.

Elsa stared at the herd, raised herself very cautiously to a crouching position, with her head on her paws, and then suddenly rushed at top speed towards the herd. There was a thundering noise and the crash of breaking wood as the buffaloes bolted with Elsa in hot pursuit.

We ran after her as fast as we could and found her facing a thicket, panting hard. From within the bush came the angry snorting of the buffaloes; they had evidently rallied and were preparing to defend their young. A moment later several enraged cows charged Elsa who, recognising her limitations, withdrew, keeping in line with George, myself and Makedde. Then she made a series of quick thrusts forward, but returned equally fast to her support.

George waited until the herd was within about fifteen yards of us, then he and Makedde shouted and each waved one arm, holding his rifle in the other. The animals were puzzled by this strange performance and after a moment of indecision turned and made off.

After a while we followed, but we took good care to make certain that no buffalo was waiting to ambush us, for they are notoriously dangerous creatures.

Next morning George had to leave; I stayed on and Elsa spent three days in camp with me in spite of the continual calling of her mate.

One evening she looked towards the river, stiffened and then rushed into the bush. A tremendous barking of baboons ensued, till it was silenced by her roars. Soon she was answered by her lion – he must have been only about fifty yards away. His voice seemed to shake the earth and increased in strength. From the other side Elsa roared back. Sitting between them, I became a little anxious in case the loving pair should decide to come into my tent, for I had no meal to offer them. However, in time they appeared to have roared themselves hoarse. Their whuffings died away and no further sound came from the bush except for the buzzing of insects. Luckily on the following evening George returned with a goat for Elsa.

2. THE BIRTH OF THE CUBS

It was now nearly mid-December and we believed that the cubs might arrive at any moment.

Elsa was so heavy that every movement seemed to require an effort; if she had been living a normal life she would certainly have taken exercise, so I did my best to make her go for walks with me, but she kept close to the tents. We wondered what place she would choose for her delivery and even thought that since she had always considered our tent as her safest 'den' the cubs might be born in it.

We therefore prepared a feeding bottle and laid in some tinned milk and some glucose, and I read all the books and pamphlets I could find on animal births and possible complications.

Since I had no experience of midwifery I felt very nervous and also asked advice of a veterinary surgeon.

We also had the fear that her lion might get tired of sharing her with us. It had taken us a very long time to find a mate for her; it would be unforgivable if our interference now caused him to leave her. We wanted her cubs to grow up as wild lions and to do this they needed their father.

We decided to go away for three days. It was of course a risk, for the cubs might be born during this time and Elsa might need us, but we thought the danger that her lion might desert her the greater of the two evils – so we left.

We returned on the 16th December and found a very hungry Elsa waiting for us. For two days she remained in camp; possibly frequent thunderstorms made her reluctant to leave its shelter. She did, however, to our surprise, take a few short walks, always to the Big Rock, but returned quickly. She ate unbelievably and we felt that she was stocking up a reserve for the days that lay ahead.

On the night of the 18th December she crept in the dark

through the thorn fence which surrounded my tent and spent the night close to my bed. This was something which she had very rarely done, and I took it as a sign that she felt that her time was near.

The next day when George and I went for a walk Elsa followed us, but she had to sit down at intervals panting and was plainly in great discomfort. When we saw this we turned back and walked very slowly. Suddenly to our astonishment she turned off into the bush in the direction of the Big Rock.

She did not return during that night, but in the morning we heard her calling in a very weak voice. We thought this meant that she had had her cubs and went out to trace her spoor. These led us close to the rock but the grass was so high that we lost track of her.

We set out again in the afternoon and eventually we spotted her through our field-glasses. She was standing on the Big Rock and from her silhouette we saw that she was still pregnant.

We climbed up and found her lying close to a large boulder which stood at the top of a wide cleft in the rock; near to it there was some grass and a small tree provided shade. This place had always been one of Elsa's favourite 'lookouts' and we felt that it would make an ideal nursery, since inside the cleft was a rain-proof and well-protected cave.

We left her to take the initiative and presently she came slowly towards us, walking very carefully and obviously in pain. She greeted us very affectionately and turned away again.

When I came near her she got up and moved to the edge of the rock, and remained there with her head turned away from us. It seemed to me that she chose this precipitous position to make sure that no one could follow her. At intervals she came back and rubbed her head very gently against mine and then walked determinedly back to the boulder making it plain that she wished to be left alone.

We went a short distance away and for half an hour watched her through our field-glasses. She rolled from side to side, and moaned repeatedly. Suddenly she rose, went very carefully down the steep rock face and disappeared into the thick bush at its base.

Since there was nothing we could do to help her, we went back to camp. After dark we heard her lion calling; there was no reply.

I lay awake most of the night thinking about her and when, towards morning, it started to rain my anxiety increased and I could hardly bear to wait till is was light to go out and try to discover what had happened.

Very early, George and I set out; first we followed the spoor of Elsa's lion. He had been close to the camp, had dragged off the very smelly carcase of the goat which Elsa had not touched for three days, and had eaten it in the bush. Then he had walked to the rock near to the place where we had seen Elsa disappear.

We wondered what we should do next. We did not want our curiosity to bring any risk to the cubs and we were aware that captive lionesses who have been disturbed soon after giving birth to cubs have been known to kill their young. We also thought that her lion might be very near, so we decided to stop our search; instead George went off and shot a large water buck to provide Elsa and her mate with plenty of food.

I, in the meantime, climbed the Big Rock and waited for an hour, listening for any sound which might give us a clue to Elsa's whereabouts. I strained my ears but all was still; finally I could bear the suspense no longer and called. There was no answer. Was Elsa dead?

Hoping that the lion's spoor might lead us to her we took up his tracks where we had left them and traced them till they reached a dry watercourse near the rock. There we left his meal thinking that if he came for it this might help us to find Elsa.

During the night we heard him roaring in the distance and were therefore surprised next morning to find his pug marks close to the camp. He had not taken any of the meat that was close to the camp but had gone to the 'kill' we had left for him near the rock. This he had dragged for at least half a mile through most difficult terrain, across ravines, rocky outcrops and dense bush. We had no wish to disturb him at his meal, so we set about looking for Elsa, but found no trace of her. After returning to the camp for breakfast we went out again and suddenly, through our field-glasses, saw a great flock of vultures perched on the trees which grew around the spot where we thought that the lion had made his meal.

Assuming that he had finished by now, we approached the place and as we came near to it found every bush and tree loaded with birds of prey. Each was staring at the dry watercourse and there was the carcase lying out in the hot sun. Since the meat was in the open and yet the vultures did not leave their perches we concluded that the lion was guarding his 'kill.' As far as we could see he had not touched it, so we thought that Elsa too might be close by and that her gallant mate had dragged the four-hundred-pound burden this long distance for her benefit. We felt it would be unwise to continue our search and went back to camp for lunch after which we set out again.

When we saw that the vultures were still on the trees, we circled the place downwind and approached it very cautiously from the high ground.

George, Makedde and I had just passed a very thick bush which overhung a deep crack in the ground when I suddenly had a strange uncomfortable feeling. I stopped and looking back, saw the Toto, who was close behind me, staring intently at the bush. Next there was a terrifying growl and the sound of snapping branches; a second later all was quiet again – the lion had gone. We had passed within six feet of him. I think that my sense of uneasiness must have been due to the fact that he had been watching our movements with great intensity. When the Toto stooped to see what was in the bush he couldn't stand it and went off. They had actually looked straight into each other's eyes and the Toto had seen his big body disappearing into the deep crack. Feeling we had been very lucky, we went home and left three lots of meat in different places before night fell.

As soon as it was light we went to inspect the deposits; all of them had been taken by hyenas.

By the river we found the spoor of Elsa's mate, but there was no sign of her pug marks. All the little rain pools had dried up long ago and the river was the only place where she could quench

18

her thirst; the absence of any trace of her was very worrying. Eventually we found, close to the spot where three days before we had last seen her, a few pug marks which could have been hers, though this was not certain. Full of hope, we made a thorough search along the base of the Big Rock, but in vain.

Since the vultures had now gone we were left with no clue to her whereabouts.

Again we put out meat close to the rock and near to the camp. In the morning we found that Elsa's lion had dragged some of it to the studio and eaten it there, while the rest had been disposed of by hyenas.

It was now four days since we had seen Elsa and six since she had eaten anything, unless she had shared the water buck with her mate.

We believed that she had given birth to the cubs on the night of the 20th December and we did not think that it could be a co-incidence that her lion, who had not been about for days, had reappeared on that night and remained close to the rock ever since, which was most unusual.

On Christmas Eve George went to get a goat while I continued the fruitless search and called to Elsa without getting any answer.

Early on Christmas morning we went in search of Elsa. We followed the lion's spoor across the river, and again screened the bush all round the spot to which he had dragged the water buck. After hours of fruitless tracking we came back for breakfast.

Later we set out once more for the rocky range; something seemed to tell us that if Elsa were still alive that was where she was. We wriggled through dense bush and I crept hopefully into every crevice trying to prevent myself from expecting to find Elsa dead but hidden from the vultures by the impenetrable thorn thickets.

When we were all tired out we sat down to rest in the shade of an overhanging rock and discussed every possible fate which might have overtaken Elsa. We were very depressed and even Nuru and Makedde spoke in subdued voices.

At midday we returned to camp and began a very gloomy and silent Christmas meal.

19

Suddenly there was a swift movement and before I could take in what was happening Elsa was between us sweeping everything off the table, knocking us to the ground, sitting on us and overwhelming us with joy and affection.

While this was going on the boys appeared and Elsa gave them too a full share of her greetings.

Her figure was normal again and she looked superbly fit. We gave her some meat which she immediately ate. Meanwhile, we discussed many questions. Why had she come to visit us during the hottest part of the day, a time when normally she would never move? Could it be that she had chosen it deliberately because it was the safest time to leave the cubs since few predators would be on the prowl in such heat. Had the cubs died? And whatever had happened, why had she waited for five days before coming to us for food?

After she had had a good meal and drunk some water she rubbed her head affectionately against us, walked about thirty yards down the river, lay down and had a doze. We left her alone, so that she should feel at ease. When I looked for her at tea-time she had gone.

We followed her spoor for a short way; it led towards the rock range, but we soon lost it and returned none the wiser about her cubs. However, now that we were reassured about Elsa our morale was restored.

During the night we heard her lion calling from the other side of the river, but she did not answer him.

We began to worry about the cubs. We felt we just must know about them. So the next morning we searched for five hours, but we did not find so much as a dropping or a crushed leaf, let alone any spoor to show where Elsa's nursery was.

We carried on equally unsuccessfully in the afternoon. While plodding through the bush George nearly stepped on an exceptionally large puff adder and was lucky to be able to shoot it just before it could strike.

Half an hour later we heard Ibrahim popping off a gun, a signal that Elsa had arrived in camp.

Obviously she had responded to the shot with which George

had dispatched the puff adder.

She was most affectionate to us when we got back and having eaten enormously, had settled down and showed no intention of returning to her cubs. This alarmed me because it was getting dark and the worst moment to leave them alone.

We tried to induce her to return to them by walking along the path down which she had come. She followed us reluctantly, listening alertly in the direction of the rock, but soon returned to camp. We wondered whether she might be afraid that we would follow her and find her cubs. Meanwhile she went back to her meal and it was only after she had methodically cleaned up every scrap of it that, much to our relief, she disappeared into the dark. Very likely she had waited till there was no light to make sure we could not follow her.

We were now convinced that she was looking after her cubs, but could not be happy until we had seen for ourselves that they were healthy and normal.

We made one more unsuccessful search before our return to Isiolo where we spent the last three days of December. On our way back to her camp we nearly collided with two rhino and then met a small herd of elephant. We had no choice but to rush past them, hoping we should 'make it,' but the big bull of the herd took umbrage and chased us for quite a long way. I did not enjoy this as elephants are the only wild animals which really frighten me.

We hooted several times before we reached camp to let Elsa know we were arriving and found her waiting for us on top of a large boulder at the point at which the track passes the end of the Big Rock.

She hopped in among the boys at the back of the Land-Rover, then she went to the trailer in which there was a dead goat. I had rarely seen her so hungry.

After she had spent seven hours in camp, eating and hopping on and off the Land-Rover, we began to be afraid that she no longer had any cubs to look after. She only left us at two in the morning.

The next day we set out and followed her spoor which led to-

21

wards the Big Rock. Close to it was what seemed to us an ideal home for a lioness and her family. Very large boulders gave complete shelter and they were surrounded by bush that was almost impenetrable. We made straight for the topmost boulder and from it tried to look down into the centre of the 'den.' We saw no pug marks but there were signs that some animal had used it as a lie-up.

This was very close to the place where we had seen Elsa in labour, so we thought that she had perhaps given birth to the cubs there. On the other hand, we had been within three feet of it on one of our previous searches and it seemed almost impossible that Elsa should have been there hiding her cubs and not made us aware of her presence.

As though to prove that we were wrong in thinking this, after we had called loudly for half an hour, she suddenly appeared out of a cluster of bush only twenty yards away. She seemed rather shocked at seeing us, stared and kept silent and very still as though hoping we would not come nearer.

Perhaps we were so close to her nursery that she thought it better to appear and so prevent us from finding it. After a few moments, she walked up to us and was very affectionate to George, myself, Makedde and the Toto, but never uttered a sound.

Soon she went slowly back towards the bush and stood, for about five minutes, with her back turned towards us listening intently for any sound from the thicket. Then she sat down, still with her back turned to us. It was as though she wanted to say to us: 'Here my private world begins and you must not trespass.'

It was a dignified demonstration and no words could have conveyed her wishes more clearly.

We sneaked away as quietly as we could, having decided that we must respect Elsa's wishes and not try to see the cubs until she brought them to us, which we felt sure she would do one day. I determined to stay on in camp in order to provide her with food so that she would have no need to leave her family unguarded for long periods while she went out hunting for them. We also decided to take her meals to her, so as to reduce the time during which she had to desert the cubs.

We put our plan into immediate operation and that afternoon went by car close to her lie-up. We knew that Elsa would associate the vibrations of the engine with us and with food.

As we neared the place where we had last seen her we started to call out – 'Maji, Chakula, Nyama' – Swahili words, meaning water, food, meat, with which Elsa was familiar.

Soon she came, was as affectionate as usual and ate a lot. While she had her head in a basin, which we had sunk in the ground to keep it steady, and was busy drinking, we went off. She looked round when she heard the engine start but made no move to follow us.

Next morning we took her her day's ration but she failed to turn up, nor was she there when we went again in the afternoon. During the night a strange lion came to within fifteen yards of our tent and removed the remains.

After breakfast we followed his spoor which led to the Big Rock and pug marks there showed that another lion had been with him. We hoped that Elsa was enjoying their company and that perhaps they were helping her with her housekeeping.

We went down to the river to see whether she had left any spoor there. She had not, but soon afterwards George, who was going to fetch another goat, met her near the rock. She was very thirsty, the aluminium drinking basin had gone and we wondered whether the other lions had stolen it. On his return George fed her and from her appetite he thought it unlikely that the lions had provided her with any of the food they had stolen.

Later in the day George went off to Isiolo. Elsa stayed in camp with me till the late afternoon, then I saw her sneak into the bush upstream and followed her. Obviously she did not wish to be observed, for when she caught my scent, she pretended to sharpen her claws on a tree. Then as soon as I turned my back on her, she jumped at me and knocked me over, as though to say, 'That's for spying on me!' Now it was my turn to pretend that I had only come to bring more meat to her. She accepted my excuse, followed me and began eating again. After this nothing would induce her to return to the cubs until long after night had

23

fallen. I was reading in my tent and she felt certain that I would not be likely to follow her.

During the following days I went on taking food to the spot near to which we believed the cubs to be. Whenever I met Elsa on these occasions, she took great pains to conceal the where-abouts of her lie-up, often doubling back on her tracks, no doubt to puzzle me.

One afternoon when I was passing the Big Rock I saw a very strange animal standing on it. In the dim light it looked like a cross between a hyena and a small lion. When it saw me it sneaked off with the gait of a cat. It had obviously spotted the cubs and I was much alarmed. Later when I brought up some food, Elsa came at once when I called her; she seemed unusually alert and was rather fierce to the Toto. I left her still eating on the roof of my truck. It was there that we placed the meat in the evening to keep it out of the reach of predators. I did not know what to do for the best. If I continued to leave food close to Elsa's nursery, would it not attract predators? Alternatively, if I kept the meat in camp and Elsa had to desert her cubs to come and fetch it, might they not be killed while she was absent? Faced with these two unsatisfactory choices, I decided, on bal-ance, to go on providing food near to her lie-up. When I did so on the following evening, I heard the growls of several lions close to me and Elsa appeared to be both nervous and very thirsty.

After this I made up my mind that in spite of her disapproval I had better find out how many cubs there were and whether they were all right. I might then be able to help in an emergency. On the 11th of January I did an unpardonable thing. I left a Game Scout (Makedde was ill) with the rifle on the road below and, accompanied by the Toto, whom Elsa knew well, I climbed the rock-face calling repeatedly to warn her of our approach. She did not answer. I told the Toto to take off his sandals so as not to make any noise.

When we had reached the top we stood on the edge of the cliff and raked the bush below with our field-glasses. Immediately under us was the place from which Elsa had emerged that first time, when we had surprised her and she had stood on guard.

Now, there was no sign of her, but the place looked like a well-used nursery and was ideal for the purpose.

Although I was concentrating very hard on my examination of the bush below us I suddenly had a strange feeling, dropped my field-glasses, turned and saw Elsa creeping up behind the Toto. I had just time to shout a warning to him before she knocked him down. She had crept up the rock behind us quite silently and the Toto only missed toppling over the cliff by a hair's breadth and that mainly because his feet were bare, which gave him the chance of getting a grip on the rock.

Next Elsa walked over to me and knocked me over in a friendly way, but it was very obvious that she was expressing annoyance at finding us so close to her cubs.

After this demonstration, she walked slowly along the crest of the rock, from time to time looking back over her shoulder to make sure that we were following her. Silently she led us to the far end of the ridge. There we climbed down into the bush. As soon as we were on level ground she rushed ahead, repeatedly turning her head back to confirm that we were coming.

In this way, she took us back to the road, but she made a wide detour, presumably to avoid passing near the cubs. I interpreted her complete silence as a wish not to alarm them or to prevent them from emerging and following us.

When we walk together I usually pat Elsa occasionally and she likes it, but to-day she would not allow me to touch her and made it clear that I was in disgrace. Even when she was eating her dinner on the roof of the car back in camp, whenever I came near her she turned away from me.

She did not go to the cubs until it was dark.

Now George came up from Isiolo and we changed guard. Elsa had made me feel that I could do no more spying on her; George had not had the same experience, so he had fewer inhibitions. My curiosity was immense and I felt that it would be a happy compromise if he did 'the wrong thing' and I were to profit by his misdeed.

3. WE SEE THE CUBS

One afternoon, while I was at our home in Isiolo a hundred miles away, George crept very quietly up Elsa's Big Rock and peered over the top.

Below he saw her suckling two cubs and as her head was hidden by an overhanging rock, he felt sure that she had not seen him. Having seen the family, George went back to camp and collected a carcase.

The brief sight George had had of the two suckling cubs had not given him time to discover whether they were normal or not and of course he could not tell whether there might be others hidden from his view. So on the afternoon of the 14th January, when Elsa was in camp feeding, he crept off to the Zom rocks, while I kept her company.

For two days she had been constantly in this area, so we supposed that she had changed the place of the nursery.

George climbed up to the top of the centre rock and inside a cleft saw three cubs; two were asleep, but the third was chewing at some Sansevieria; it looked up at him but as its eyes were still blurred and bluish he did not think that it could focus well enough to see him.

He took four photographs but did not expect to get good prints for the cleft in which the cubs lay was rather dark. While he was doing this the two cubs who had been sleeping woke up and crawled about. It seemed to him that they were perfectly healthy.

When he came back to camp and told me the excellent news, Elsa was still there and quite unsuspicious.

At dusk we drove her near to the Zom rocks. But only after we had tactfully walked away and she was reassured by hearing our voices fading into the distance did she jump off the Land-Rover and, presumably, rejoin the cubs.

George now went back to Isiolo. The morning after he had left I heard Elsa's mate calling from the other side of the river but I listened in vain for her reply. In the afternoon, however, she roared very loudly quite near to the camp and went on doing so until I joined her. She seemed overjoyed at seeing me and came back to camp with me, but ate very little and went off when it became dark.

On a February afternoon while I was writing in the studio (a place on the river-bank overhung by the branches of a large tree where I work), the Toto came running to tell me that Elsa was calling in a very strange voice from the other side of the river. I went upstream following the sound, till I broke through the undergrowth at a place close to camp, where in the dry season there is a fairly wide sandbank on our side and on the other a dry watercourse which drops abruptly into the river.

Suddenly I stopped unable to believe my eyes.

There was Elsa standing on the sandbank within a few yards of me, one cub close to her, a second cub emerging from the water shaking itself dry and the third one still on the far bank, pacing to and fro and calling piteously. Elsa looked fixedly at me, her expression a mixture of pride and embarrassment.

I remained absolutely still while she gave a gentle moan to her young, that sounded like *M – hm, M – hm*; then she walked up to the landing cub, licked it affectionately and turned back to the river to go to the youngster who was stranded on the far bank. The two cubs who had come across with her followed her immediately, swimming bravely through the deep water, and soon the family were reunited.

Near to where they landed a fig tree grows out of some rocks, whose grey roots grip the stone like a net; Elsa rested in its shade, her golden coat showing up vividly against the dark green foliage and the silver-grey boulders. At first the cubs hid, but soon their curiosity got the better of their shyness. They began by peeping cautiously at me through the undergrowth and then came out into the open and stared inquisitively.

Elsa *M – hm, M – hm*'d which reassured them and when they were quite at their ease they began to climb on to their mother's back and tried to catch her switching tail. Rolling affectionately over her, exploring the rocks and squeezing their fat little tum-

27

mies under the roots of the fig tree, they forgot all about me.

After a while Elsa rose and went to the water's edge intending to enter the river again; one cub was close to her and plainly meant to follow her.

Unfortunately, at this moment the Toto, whom I had sent back to fetch Elsa's food, arrived with it. Immediately she flattened her ears and remained immobile until the boy had dropped the meat and gone away. Then she swam quickly across followed by one cub, which, though it kept close to her, seemed to be quite unafraid of the water. When Elsa settled down to her meal, the plucky little fellow turned back and started to swim over on its own to join, or perhaps to help, the other two cubs.

As soon as Elsa saw it swimming out of its depth, she plunged into the river, caught up with it, grabbed its head in her mouth and ducked it so thoroughly that I was quite worried about the little thing.

When she had given it a lesson not to be too venturesome, she retrieved it and brought it, dangling out of her mouth, to our bank.

By this time a second cub plucked up courage and swam across, its tiny head just visible above the rippling water, but the third stayed on the far bank looking frightened.

Elsa came up to me and began rolling on her back and showing her affection for me; it seemed that she wanted to prove to her cubs that I was part of the pride and could be trusted.

Reassured, the two cubs crept cautiously closer and closer, their large expressive eyes watching Elsa's every movement and mine, till they were within three feet of me. I found it difficult to restrain an impulse to lean forward and touch them, but I remembered the warning a zoologist had given me: Never touch cubs unless they take the initiative, and this three-foot limit seemed to be an invisible boundary which they felt that they must not cross.

While all this was happening the third cub kept up a pathetic miaowing from the far bank, appealing for help.

Elsa watched it for a time, then she walked to the water's edge, at the point at which the river is narrowest. With the two brave cubs cuddling beside her she called to the timid one to join them. But its only response was to pace nervously up and down; it was too frightened to try to cross.

When Elsa saw it was so distressed she went to its rescue accompanied by the two bold ones who seemed to enjoy swimming.

Soon they were all on the opposite side again where they had a wonderful time climbing up the steep bank of a sand lugga, which runs into the river, rolling down it, landing on each other's backs and balancing on the trunk of a fallen doam palm.

Elsa licked them affectionately, talked to them in her soft moaning voice, never let them out of her sight and whenever one ventured too far off for her liking, went after the explorer and brought it back.

I watched them for about an hour and then called Elsa who replied in her usual voice, which was quite different from the one she used when talking to the cubs.

She came down to the water's edge, waited till all her family were at her feet and started to swim across. This time all three cubs came with her.

As soon as they had landed she licked each one in turn and then, instead of charging up to me as she usually does when coming out of the river, she walked up slowly, rubbed herself gently against me, rolled in the sand, licked my face and finally hugged me. I was very much moved by her obvious wish to show her cubs that we were friends. They watched us from a distance, interested, but puzzled and determined to stay out of reach.

Next Elsa and the cubs went to the carcase, which she started eating, while the youngsters licked the skin and tore at it, somersaulted over it and became very excited. It was probably their first encounter with a 'kill.'

The evidence suggested that they were six weeks and two days old. They were in excellent condition and though they still had a bluish film over their eyes they could certainly see perfectly. Their coats had fewer spots than Elsa's or her sisters', and were also very much less thick than theirs had been at the same age, but far finer and more shiny. I could not tell their sex, but I noticed imediately that the cub with the lightest coat was much

29

livelier and more inquisitive than the other two and especially devoted to its mother. It always cuddled close up to her, if possible under her chin and embraced her with its little paws. Elsa was very gentle and patient with her family and allowed them to crawl all over her and chew her ears and tail.

Gradually she moved closer to me and seemed to be inviting me to join in their game. But when I wriggled my fingers in the sand the cubs, though they cocked their round foxy faces, kept their distance.

When it got dark Elsa listened attentively and then took the cubs some yards into the bush. A few moments later I heard the sound of suckling.

I returned to camp and when I arrived it was wonderful to find Elsa and the cubs waiting for me about ten yards from the tent.

I patted her and she licked my hand. Then I called the Toto and together we brought the remains of the carcase up from the river. Elsa watched us and it seemed to me that she was pleased that we were relieving her of the task of pulling the heavy load. But, when we came within twenty yards of her, she suddenly rushed at us with flattened ears. I told the boy to drop the meat and remain still and I began to drag it near to the cubs. When she saw that I was handling the 'kill' alone, Elsa was reassured and as soon as I deposited it she started eating. After watching her for a while, I went to my tent and was surprised to see her following me. She flung herself on the ground and called to the cubs to come and join me. But they remained outside miaowing; soon she went back to them and so did I.

We all sat together on the grass, Elsa leaning against me while she suckled her family.

The evening was very peaceful, the moon rose slowly and the doam palms were silhouetted against the light; there was not a sound except for the suckling of the cubs.

So many people had warned me that after Elsa's cubs had been born she would probably turn into a fierce and dangerous mother defending her young, yet here she was as trusting and affectionate as ever, and wanting me to share her happiness. I felt very humble.

30

4. THE CUBS IN CAMP

When I woke up next morning there was no sign of Elsa or the cubs, and as it had rained during the night all spoor had been washed away.

About tea-time she turned up alone, very hungry; I held her meat while she chewed it so as to keep her attention and meanwhile told the Toto to follow her fresh pug marks to get a clue to the present whereabouts of the cubs.

When he returned Elsa hopped on to the roof of my car, and from this platform she watched the two of us walking back along her tracks into the bush.

I did this deliberately to induce her to return to the cubs. When she realised where we were going she promptly followed us, and, taking the lead, trotted quickly along her pug marks; several times she waited till, panting, we caught up with her. I wondered whether at last she meant to take us to her lie-up. When we reached the 'Whuffing Rock,' so named because it was there that we had once surprised her with her mate and had been startled by their alarming whuffing, she stopped, listened, climbed swiftly half-way up the slope, hesitated until I had caught up with her and then rushed ahead till she had reached the saddle of the rock from which the big cleft breaks off on the far side. There, much out of breath, I joined her. I was about to pat her when she flattened her ears, and with an angry snarl gave me a heavy clout. Since it was plain that I was not wanted, I retreated. When I had gone half-way down the face of the rock I looked back and saw Elsa with one cub, while another was emerging from the cleft.

I was puzzled at the sudden change in her behaviour, but I respected her wishes and left her and her family alone. I joined the Toto who had waited in the bush just below and we watched

Elsa through our field-glasses. As soon as she saw that we were at a safe distance she relaxed and began playing with her cubs.

One cub was certainly much more attached to her than the others; it often sat between her front paws and rubbed its head against her chin, while the two others busily investigated their surroundings.

George returned on the 4th February and was delighted to hear the good news of the cubs; in the afternoon we walked towards the Whuffing Rock hoping that he too might see them.

On our way we heard the agitated barking of baboons. We thought it very likely that Elsa's presence was the cause of the commotion, so, as we approached the river, we called out to her. She appeared immediately, but though she was very friendly she was obviously upset and rushed nervously backwards and forwards between us and the bush, which grew along the river's edge. She seemed to be doing her best to prevent us from reaching the water.

We assumed that her cubs were there and were surprised that she should try to prevent George from seeing them. In the end she led us back to the camp by a wide detour.

Two days later we saw her near the Whuffing Rock. As we were walking towards it we talked rather loudly to give her notice of our approach. She emerged from the thick undergrowth at the mouth of the cleft and stood very still, gazing at us. After a few moments she sat down facing us – we were still some two hundred yards away – and made it very plain that we were not to come any nearer. Several times she turned her head towards the cleft and listened attentively, but apart from this she remained in her 'guarding' position.

We now realised that she made a difference between bringing the cubs to see us and our visiting them.

Two weeks passed before she brought the cubs to camp to introduce them to George. This was not entirely her fault for during this time we were obliged to go to Isiolo for a couple of days and while we were away she and the cubs had arrived at the camp one morning looking for us, but had found only the boys.

Makedde told us that he had gone to meet her and she had

32

rubbed her head against his legs while one plucky cub had boldly walked up to within a short distance of him.

However, when he squatted and tried to pat it, it had snarled and run off to join the others who were hiding some distance away. They had stayed in camp till lunch-time and then left.

I arrived about an hour after she had gone. Makedde was delighted with the plucky cub; he said he was sure it was a male and told me he had given it a name, which was, he said, very popular with the Meru tribe. It sounded like Jespah, which means 'God sets free.' If that were the origin of the little cub's name it could not be more appropriate. Later, when we knew that the family consisted of two lions and a lioness, we called Jespah's brother, who was very timid, Gopa, for in Swahili this means timid, and his sister we named Little Elsa.

One drizzly morning I woke up to hear Elsa's typical cub moan coming from across the river; I jumped out of bed and was just in time to see her crossing the river with her cubs, Jespah close to her and the other two some way behind.

She walked slowly up to me, licked me and sat down next to me. Then she called repeatedly to the cubs. Jespah ventured fairly near to me, but the others kept their distance. I collected some meat which Elsa promptly dragged into a nearby bush; she and the cubs spent the next two hours eating it, while I sat on a sandbank watching them.

While they ate Elsa talked continuously to the cubs in a series of low moans. They often suckled, but also chewed at the meat.

After a while I went off to have breakfast and soon afterwards saw Elsa leading the cubs in a wide circle to the car track. I followed slowly hoping to take some photographs but she stopped suddenly broadside across the road and flattened her ears. I accepted the reproof and went back, turned to have a last look at them and saw the cubs bouncing along behind their mother going in the direction of the Big Rock. By now they were about nine weeks old and lively walkers, chasing and prodding one another as they tried to keep pace with Elsa. In spite of their high spirits they were most obedient to her call.

During the next few days Elsa often came alone to visit us. She was always affectionate but some of her habits had altered since she had given birth to the cubs. She now very seldom ambushed us, was less playful, more dignified.

I wondered where she placed her cubs when she came out on these long visits. Did she instruct them not to move till she returned? Did she hide them in a very safe spot?

When, on 19th February, George came 'on duty,' I returned to Isiolo to meet Lord William Percy and his wife to bring them to see Elsa's family.

The next day, while we were having tea in the studio, Elsa appeared alone; our friends were included in her customary friendly rubbings and she bore with my taking a few photographs, but then walked out of the picture.

She never liked being photographed and since the arrival of the cubs she had become even more averse to it.

Later, Lady William started sketching her and this was another thing she usually disliked, but to-day she seemed to have no objection. All the same, I kept close by in case she might suddenly take a dislike to serving as a model. However, as she appeared quite indifferent to what was going on, after a while I went away. As soon as my back was turned she rushed like lightning at the artist and embraced her playfully. As Elsa weighs about three hundred pounds I admired the calm way in which Lady William accepted the demonstration. After this we decided that the sketching had better cease. Elsa left us at dusk; soon a leopard began coughing and Elsa and her mate started up a lively conversation which lasted throughout most of the night.

At tea-time the next day we saw Elsa and the cubs on the opposite side of the river, but when she spotted us she moved her family a short distance downstream, then they crossed the river. We quickly fetched some meat which Elsa promptly collected and then took into the bush to her cubs who were out of sight.

Later, they all got thirsty and came to the water's edge to drink. I was glad that our guests should have this splendid view of them drinking close together, their heads stretched forward between the pointed elbows of their front legs, which were bent. At first they just lapped noisily, then they plunged into the shallow water and began to play. They were certainly not water-shy, as cats are said to be. A big boulder surrounded by water made a perfect setting for playing 'king of the castle.'

Early one morning Elsa visited the camp before anyone was up. I heard her and followed her. She was already in the water when I called to her, but she came back at once, settled with me on a sandbank and began to miaow at the cubs, encouraging them to come near us. They approached within three yards but obviously did not wish to be handled, and as the last thing I wanted was that they should become tame, I was very pleased about this.

Elsa seemed puzzled that they should still be scared of me, but in the end she gave up her attempt to make us fraternise, took her family across the river and disappeared into the bush.

That evening we found Elsa and the cubs in camp enjoying their dinner. We were silent for we knew how sensitive the cubs were to the sound of talking. They did not mind the chatter of the boys, far away in the kitchen, but if we were near them and said a word to each other, even in a low voice, they sneaked away. As for the clicking of a camera shutter – it gave them the jitters.

They were ten weeks old and Elsa had begun to wean them. Whenever she thought they had had enough milk she either sat on her teats or jumped on to the roof of the Land-Rover. So if the cubs did not want to starve they had to eat meat. They tore the intestines of the 'kills' out of their mother's mouth and sucked them in like spaghetti, through closed teeth, pressing out the un-wanted contents, just as she did.

That evening one cub was determined to get some more milk and persistently pushed its way under Elsa's belly until she became really angry, gave it a good spank and jumped on to the car.

The little ones resented this very much; they stood on their hind legs resting their forepaws against the car, miaowing up at their mother, but she sat and licked her paws, as though she were quite unaware of the whimpering cubs below.

When they had recovered from their disappointment they bounced off, cheerfully making explorations which took them out

35

of her sight. Elsa became extremely alert if they did not come when she called them, and if they did not reappear quickly she hopped off the car and fetched them back to safety.

The next two evenings Elsa came to camp without her family. She was exuberantly affectionate to all of us and swept the table clear of our drinks, which made our friends appreciate why in camp we use crockery and glasses made of unbreakable material. On the third evening, she brought the cubs with her and behaved in the same way. We were rather surprised to observe that the cubs were not in the least startled when our supper landed on the ground with a noisy clatter.

They now seemed quite at home in our presence, so it astonished us that on the two following evenings Elsa left them at an open salt lick about a hundred yards away, and we were also puzzled to know how she trained them to stay put while she enjoyed a good meal in full view of them.

During all that night it poured without stopping. On such occasions Elsa always takes refuge in George's tent, and now, in she came, calling to the cubs to follow her. But they remained outside apparently enjoying the deluge and soon their poor mother felt it her duty to go out and join them. We heard them playing round the camp and then we thought we heard muffled voices, but the drumming of the rain on the roof of our tent was so loud that it took us a little while before we realised that these were those of our friends. Their tent had collapsed and they were trying to struggle out from beneath the wet canvas.

We went to their help, hoping that Elsa and her cubs would not join the rescue team. Luckily they didn't, and while we hammered in the tent pegs and flashed our torches Elsa stood aside miaowing gently to reassure the cubs. At dawn the rain stopped and she took her family off towards the rock, and we dried our friends' clothes.

For several nights we had terrific thunderstorms and the lightning and the crashes came so close together that I was quite frightened.

As George had gone to Isiolo his tent was empty, so Elsa and the cubs could very well have sheltered in it, but the youngsters'

inbred fear of man was so great that they preferred to soak outside. This trait was the most obvious sign of their wild blood and
it was something we were determined to encourage, even at the
expense of a wetting and even in defiance of Elsa's wish to make
them into friends of ours. Often she seemed to be playing a sort
of 'catch as catch can' with them, circling nearer and nearer to
the tent in which I was sitting, as though she wanted to bring
them into it without their becoming aware of what was happening.

Twice she dashed into the tent and peeping over my shoulder
called to them. But whatever she did they never overstepped their
self-imposed frontier.

It seemed that our rearing of their mother in domesticity had
in no way impaired the instinct which all wild animals possess
and which warns them against approaching an unknown danger.
Moreover, Elsa herself had shown by concealing her cubs from
us for five or six weeks, that her own instinct for protecting her
young was still alive.

Now, she was plainly disappointed that her efforts to make one
pride of us were proving unsuccessful, partly owing to the cubs'
fear of man and partly owing to what she must have taken as
heartless lack of co-operation on our part. She seemed very
puzzled, but had no intention of giving up her plan. One evening
she entered my tent, deliberately lay down behind me and then
called softly to the cubs inviting them to suckle her. By doing this
she tried not only to make the cubs come into the tent but also to
force them to pass close to me. No doubt they would have been
pleased if I had retired behind their mother and she would have
been pleased if I had done something to encourage them, but I
remained where I was and kept still. To have moved would have
defeated Elsa's intention and to have encouraged them would
have been against our determination not to tame them. I was
sorry because I longed to help the cubs and felt distressed when
Elsa looked at me for a long time with a disappointed expression
in her eyes and then went out to join her children. Of course she
could not understand that my lack of response was due to our
wish to preserve the cubs' wild instinct. She plainly thought me

unfeeling, whereas I was suppressing all my feelings for the good of her family.

The cubs were worried about our relationship for the opposite reason and became anxious every evening when Elsa, persecuted by tsetse flies, flung herself in front of me, asking me to dispose of these pests.

When I started squashing the flies and in the process slapping Elsa, the cubs were very upset. Jespah in particular would come close and crouch, ready to spring should his mother be in need of protection. No doubt they found it odd that she should seem grateful for my slappings.

On one occasion when Elsa, Jespah and Little Elsa were drinking in front of the tent Gopa was too nervous to come to the water bowl. Seeing this, Elsa went to him with great deliberation and cuffed him several times, after which he plucked up enough courage to join the others.

Jespah's character was quite different – he was rather too brave. One afternoon after they had all fed and when their bellies were near bursting point Elsa started off towards the rock. By then it was nearly dark. Two cubs followed obediently but Jespah went on gorging. Elsa called twice to him, but he merely listened for a moment and then went on feeding. Finally, his mother came back, and it was in no uncertain manner that she walked up to her son. Jespah realised that he was in for trouble, so gobbling the meat and with large bits of it hanging out of either side of his mouth, trotted after her.

At this time I had to go for a few days to Isiolo while George came to look after the camp.

The way in which the cubs were developing into true wild lions exceeded our hopes, but their father was a great disappointment to us.

No doubt we were partly to blame, for we had interfered with his relationship with his family – but certainly he was of no help as a provider of food for them; on the contrary, he often stole their meat. Moreover, he caused us a lot of trouble. One evening he made a determined attempt to get at a goat which was inside my truck, and another time when Elsa and the cubs were eating outside our tent she suddenly scented him, became very nervous, sniffed repeatedly towards the bush, cut her meal short and hurriedly removed the cubs.

The cubs, unlike their mother, had never had any man-made toys to play with, but they wrestled in the bright lamplight and were never at a loss to find a stick to fight for when they came to camp in the evenings. At other times they played hide-and-seek and 'ambushes.' Often they would get locked in a clinch, the victim struggling on his back with all four paws in the air. Elsa usually joined in their games; in spite of her great weight, she sprang and hopped about as though she were herself a cub.

We had provided two water bowls for them, a strong aluminium basin and an old steel helmet mounted on a piece of wood, which Elsa had used since her youth. This was the more popular of the two with the cubs. They often tipped it over and were alarmed at the clatter it made when it fell. Then recovering from their fright they faced the shiny moving object with cocked heads and finally began to prod it cautiously. We took flashlight photographs of these games.

On 2nd April George went back to Isiolo but I stayed on in camp.

As the days passed I observed that the cubs were getting more and more shy even of me. Now they preferred to sneak through the grass in a wide circle to reach their meat, rather than follow their mother in a straight line, because this involved coming very close to me.

To prevent predators from stealing the meat during the night I started dragging the carcase from the doam palm near to my tent, to which I attached it by a chain.

It was often a heavy load and Elsa used to watch me apparently content that I had taken on the laborious task of protecting her meat.

Jespah was much less happy when he saw me handling the 'kill.' After several half-hearted attacks he sometimes charged me in a proper fashion, first crouching low and then rushing forward at full speed. Elsa came instantly to my rescue: she not only placed herself between her son and me, but gave him a sound and

39

deliberate cuff. Afterwards she sat with me in the tent for a long time, totally ignoring Jespah, who rested outside looking bewildered. He lay by the helmet bowl, his head against it, occasionally lapping lazily.

Touched as I was by Elsa's reaction, I also understood that Jespah should be disconcerted by his mother's disapproval of his instinctive reaction and I was most anxious not to arouse his jealousy.

He was still too small to do very much harm but we both recognised that it was essential to establish a friendly truce with the cubs while they were still dependent upon us for food and before they had grown big enough to be dangerous. It was a difficult problem because while we did not want them to be hostile, neither did we want them to become tame. Recently Elsa herself seemed to have become aware of our difficulty and to be making her contribution to solving it. While she spanked Jespah if in his attempts to protect her he attacked me, she also dealt firmly with me if she thought I was getting too familiar with her children. For instance, several times when I came close to them while they were at play, she looked at me through half-closed eyes, walked slowly but purposefully up to me, and gripped me round the knees in a friendly but determined manner, which indicated very plainly that her grip would become much firmer if I did not take the hint and retire.

5. THE PERSONALITY OF THE CUBS

One evening we tied up a carcase near our tent. Elsa soon came for her meal and did all she could to induce the cubs to join her. She pranced round and did her best to cajole them, trying by every means to break down their fear, but not even Jespah ventured into the lamplight. That evening we heard their father calling and by the next morning they had all gone.

When George left for Isiolo I stayed on. One night Elsa turned up and spent that evening resting her head against my shoulder and '*mhn-mhning*' to the cubs, a very sonorous sound, although it came through closed lips; fruitlessly, she tried to make them come to me.

I was always touched by the way in which she discriminated when she played with me or with them. With the cubs she was often rather rough, pulling their skin, biting them affectionately or holding their heads down so that they should not interfere with her meal; it would have been most painful if she had treated me in the same way, but she was always gentle when we played together.

That night it rained. In the morning I was much surprised to see not only Elsa's pug marks, but those of a cub inside George's empty tent. It was the first time that one had entered the self-imposed forbidden area.

On the following night Elsa, observing that the boys had forgotten to place thorn branches in front of the entrance to my enclosure, pushed the wicker gate aside, entered the tent and promptly lay down on my bed. Wrapped up in the torn mosquito netting she looked so content that I saw myself having to spend the night sitting in the open.

Jespah followed his mother into the tent and stood on his hind legs examining the bed, but fortunately decided against trying it out. The other cubs stayed outside. We spent most of the evening

41

trying to lure Elsa out of my tent – it was a difficult task since we dared not open the door in case all the cubs were to rush in and join their mother.

The cubs were about sixteen weeks old and by now the family should have been guarding its kill. Had Elsa become so lazy that she expected us not only to provide her with food but also to relieve her of the task of protecting it?

Were we ruining her wild instincts and should we leave her? The moment did not seem a propitious one for deserting her, because we had recently found the footprints of two strange Africans very near the camp. No doubt they had been reconnoitring our whereabouts, for the drought was again with us and probably they intended to bring their stock into the game reserves to graze, though this was illegal. In the circumstances, I felt I must go on providing the family with food; if not, Elsa would surely kill some trespassing goat. I comforted myself with the thought that very soon the rains would come, the tribesmen would go away and by the next dry season Elsa would have the cubs well on the run to hunt with her.

The cubs were very easily distinguishable. Jespah was much the lightest in colour, his body was perfectly proportioned and he had a very pointed nose and eyes so acutely slanted that they gave a slightly Mongolian cast to his sensitive face. His character was not only the most nonchalant, daring and inquisitive, but also the most affectionate. When he was not cuddling up against his mother and clasping her with his paws he demonstrated his affection to his brother and sister.

When Elsa ate I often saw him pretending to eat too, but in fact only rubbing himself against her. He followed her every-where like a shadow. His timid brother Gopa was also most attractive; he had very dark markings on his forehead but his eyes, instead of being bright and open like Jespah's, were rather clouded and squinted a little. He was bigger and more heavily built than his brother and so pot-bellied that at one time I even feared he might have a rupture. Though he was by no means stupid, he took a long time to make up his mind and, unlike Jespah, was not venturesome; indeed, he always stayed behind till he was satisfied that all was safe.

Little Elsa fitted her name, for she was a replica of her mother at the same age. She had the same expression, the same markings, the same slender build. Her behaviour, too, was so strikingly like Elsa's that we could only hope that she would develop the same lovable character.

She knew of course that for the moment she was at a disadvantage compared to her two stronger brothers, but she used cunning to restore the balance. Though all the cubs were well disciplined and obeyed Elsa instantly on all important occasions, when playing they showed no fear of her and were only occasionally intimidated by the cuffs she gave them when they became too cheeky.

By the time the cubs were eighteen weeks old Elsa seemed to have become resigned to the fact that their relationship with us would never be the same as ours with her.

Indeed, they were growing more shy every day and preferred to eat outside the area lit by our lamp, except for Jespah, who, as he followed his mother everywhere, often came with her into the 'danger zone.' Elsa now often placed herself between us and the cubs in a defensive position.

As they were in excellent condition we thought that we should risk leaving them to hunt with Elsa, anyway, for a few days. Their father had been about lately and as the family had only come into camp for short feeding visits, we assumed that they were spending most of their time with him.

While the boys were breaking camp I went to the studio, and sitting on the ground, with my back against a tree, started reading a huge bundle of letters from readers of *Born Free*. They had come up with the Land-Rover which had arrived to transport our belongings. I was worrying about how I should find time to answer them all, as I wanted to, when suddenly I was squashed by Elsa. As I struggled to free myself from beneath her three hundred pounds the letters were scattered all round the place and, when I had got on to my feet again and began to collect them, Elsa bounced on to me every time I bent down to pick one up and we rolled together on the ground. The cubs thought this

43

splendid fun and dashed round after the fluttering paper. I thought that Elsa's admirers would have enjoyed seeing how much their letters were appreciated. In the end, I am glad to say that I recovered every one of them; I sent for Elsa's dinner and this diverted her attention and that of the cubs.

By this time the boys had finished packing and the loaded cars were waiting some distance away.

In spite of the loud noise of the cataracts Elsa at once heard the vibrations of the engines. She listened alertly and then looked up at me, her pupils widely dilated, so that her eyes seemed almost black. I had a strong impression that as on previous occasions she realised we were about to desert her and her expression seemed to say: 'What do you mean by leaving me and my cubs without food?' Then she abandoned her half-eaten meal, moved slowly down the sandy lugga with her children and disappeared.

On our return to Isiolo we were thrilled to hear that a call from London had come through three times in the last few days and was now booked for the next morning.

To speak to someone in England, four thousand miles away, is very exciting when one is in a remote outpost. The voice we heard was that of Billy Collins accepting our invitation to come out and meet Elsa. For his arrival we fixed a day during the following week; this would make it possible for him to be with us on our next visit to Elsa.

We chartered a plane to bring him from Nairobi to the nearest place at which an aeroplane can land and then, two days beforehand, we set off. We were determined to find Elsa and try to keep her and the cubs near to the camp so that she should be there to meet her publisher.

When we arrived in camp, George fired a shot to notify Elsa of the fact, and soon we heard her '*hnk-hnk*' but she did not turn up. As her voice came from the direction of the studio, I went to it and saw her and the cubs by the river drinking. She glanced at me and went on lapping, as though she were not in the least surprised to see me after eight days' absence.

But later she came up and licked me, and Jespah settled himself about a foot away; then she sprang on to the table and lay stretched at full length on it. Jespah stood on his hind legs and rubbed noses with her. Though they ate a little of the meat I had brought them, they did not seem hungry. However, when George tried to rescue the remains of the carcase, Elsa pulled it gently away from him and took it into a thicket. During the evening we heard Elsa's mate calling and around midnight George woke up to find her sitting on his bed and licking him, while the cubs sat outside the tent watching her.

In the morning I set off with Ibrahim, Makedde and the cook to meet Billy Collins. We took camping equipment with us, for we were not sure when he would arrive and had to provide for the possibility of having to spend a night in the bush on our return journey. When we passed the Big Rock I saw Elsa outlined on its top, watching us drive away. After we had gone about five miles we met a herd of some thirty elephants, which had several young calves with them. Luckily they had crossed the car track just before we arrived and were moving steadily away from us.

We had left very early and in consequence saw an unusual amount of game, bush buck, zebra, water buck, gerenuk and warthogs which kept to the bush while herds of Grant gazelles, impala and eland grazed on the open plain.

We were not surprised to see the eland as they always keep to the same area and we knew this herd well. There were ostriches, too, and enormous flocks of guinea fowl chasing each other about over the lava and looking like rolling stones. Most amusing were the baboons, standing up like ninepins in the long grass to get a better view of us. I could only wish that all these lovely animals would be there when we came back so that our guest should see them, though I hoped I might be spared introducing him to the elephants, at least until George was with us.

At lunch-time we arrived in the little Somali village where we expected the aeroplane to land, and I told the Africans to keep the airstrip free of livestock, as a plane might arrive at any moment.

About tea-time we heard the vibrations of an engine, but it was

45

a long time before the circling aircraft landed. Then the airstrip was suddenly covered by the entire village population, chattering excitedly. The colourful turbaned Mohammedans, clad in loose-falling garments, watched Billy Collins and the pilot clamber out from the small cabin.

We set off immediately and after many hours of brushing and winding our car through thick bush, we arrived at camp, ready for a reviving drink but before George had time to pour it out we heard the familiar '*hnk-hnk*' and a few moments later Elsa came rushing along, followed by her cubs. She welcomed us in her usual friendly manner and after a few cautious sniffs also rubbed her head against Billy, while the cubs watched from a short distance. Then she took the meat and dragged it out of the lamplight into the dark near my tent, where she settled with her children for their meal. While this went on we had our supper. We had made a special thorn enclosure next to George's tent for Billy's tent and after introducing him to his home, barricaded his wicker gate from outside with thorns and left him to a well-deserved night's sleep.

Elsa remained outside my tent enclosure and I heard her softly talking to her cubs, until I fell asleep. At dawn I was woken by noises from Billy's tent and recognised his voice and George's: evidently they were trying to persuade Elsa to leave Billy's bed. As soon as it got light she had squeezed herself through the densely woven wicker gate and hopped on to Billy's bed, caress-ing him affectionately through the torn mosquito net and holding him prisoner under her heavy body. Billy kept admirably calm considering that it was his first experience of waking up with a fully-grown lioness resting on him. Even when Elsa nibbled him slightly in his arm, her way of showing her affection, he did nothing but talk quietly to her.

Soon she lost interest and followed George out of the enclosure where she romped round the tents with her cubs as if her visit to Billy had only been a morning call on her new friend. Afterwards the family disappeared towards the Big Rock.

After tea we drove to the Big Rock where we found Elsa on its top posing magnificently against the sky. We walked to the base of the rock, hoping to film Elsa and her cubs. Elsa watched our every step, but never moved, however coaxingly we called to her. She kept aloof, and the cubs did not appear. We waited for a considerable time but as nothing happened we decided to try our luck with a herd of elephants that George had spotted earlier.

As soon as we had returned to the car Elsa stood up and called her cubs; as if to tease us, all of them now posed splendidly. We had been waiting for over one hour for just this. However, as Elsa had made it so clear that she was in no mood to be filmed, we drove on to the spot where George had met the elephants, but we found nothing but their footmarks and we returned to Elsa.

By the time we reached the rock the light was too weak for photographing, so we just watched the family through our field-glasses. The cubs chased and ambushed each other round the boulders while Elsa kept her eyes fixed on us. Finally, we called her and she came down at once, rushed through the bush and, after greeting us all affectionately, landed with a heavy thud on the roof of the Land-Rover. While we patted her paws which dangled over the windscreen, she watched the cubs which were still playing on the rock quite unconcerned at her departure. Though Elsa seemed to enjoy our attentions, she never took her eyes off her children until they finally scrambled down the rock. Then she jumped off the car and disappeared into the bush to meet them.

We took this opportunity to drive home and prepare a carcase for the family. As soon as it was ready they arrived and began to tear at the meat, while we had our drinks a few feet away. All that evening we watched the lions who seemed to have accepted Billy as a friend.

Before daybreak I was again woken up by noises coming from his tent, into which Elsa had once more found her way to say good morning. After some coaxing from George, who had come to his rescue, she left. George then reinforced the thorns outside the wicker gate with such a bulk that he felt sure Elsa would not be able to penetrate this barricade, so he went to bed again. But Elsa was not going to be defeated by a few thorns and so after a short time Billy found himself again being embraced by her and squashed under her weight. While he struggled to free himself from the entangling mosquito net George came to his rescue, but this time he took much longer to remove the thorns outside the gate, and by the time he got inside Elsa had managed to clasp her paws around Billy's neck and held his cheekbones between her teeth. We had often watched her doing this to her cubs; it was a sign of affection, but the effect on Billy must have been very different. It was very remarkable that he did not lose his head. By the time I arrived Elsa had left the tent and was playing with her cubs near the river bush.

I was very much alarmed at Elsa's unusual behaviour. She had never done anything like this to a visitor and I could only interpret it as a sign of affection; if she had not done it in play she could have acted in a very different way, but whatever her motive may have been, I was very upset and remained with Billy in his tent until Elsa, I hoped, had taken her cubs away for the day. In spite of my precaution she forced herself a third time through the wicker gate before either George who was outside or I who was inside could stop her. Billy was standing up this time and, being tall and strong, braced himself against Elsa's weight when she stood on her hind legs, resting her front paws on his shoulders, and nibbled at his ear. As soon as she released him I gave her such a beating that she sulkily left the tent and in a rather embarrassed way spent her affection now on Jespah, rolling with him in the grass, biting and clasping him exactly as she had done Billy. Finally, the whole family gambolled off towards the rocks. I do not know who was more shaken – poor Billy or myself. All we could think was that this extraordinary reaction of Elsa to Billy was her way of accepting him into the family, for only to her cubs and to us had she ever shown her affection in this way. Had she been jealous of Billy or disliked him she could easily have hurt him. We certainly did not want to risk a repetition of her demonstrations towards our friend, so we decided to break his visit short and leave camp immediately after breakfast.

'The third cub kept up a pathetic miawing from the far bank'

'She brought it, dangling out of her mouth, to our bank'

A visit from
the family

Elsa suckling
her cubs

Opposite. 'They
began by peeping
cautiously at me
through the
undergrowth'

Elsa and Jespah

The cubs enjoying their meal

A peaceful moment for Elsa and Joy

Elsa nuzzles one of her cubs

The cubs chewed one another happily

Interruption

The family enjoy a cooling swim

Elsa and Jespah
help George to write
his Christmas cards

Jespah inspects
Makedde's rifle

Jespah, Gopa and Little Elsa

A water game

Elsa gives a lesson in combat

A hungry family

Jespah could not always be relied upon
to retract his claws

Living Free

6. THE CAMP IS BURNED

At the beginning of June, after ten days' absence, we returned to camp and, just before sunset, reached a place about six miles short of it. We saw that every tree and bush was loaded with birds of prey, and drove slowly towards them. Then suddenly we found ourselves surrounded by elephant who had closed in on us from every direction. It must have been the herd, numbering some thirty or forty head, which had been in the neighbourhood for the past weeks. They had a large number of very young calves with them whose worried mothers came close to the car with raised trunks and fanning ears, shaking their heads angrily at us. It was a tricky situation and it was not improved by the arrival of my truck which, driven by Ibrahim, was following close behind us. George at once jumped on to the roof of the Land-Rover and stood there, rifle in hand. We waited for what seemed an endless time, then some of the elephants started to cross the car track about twenty yards from us.

It was a magnificent sight. The giants moved in single file, jerking their massive heads disapprovingly in our direction; to protect their young they kept them closely wedged between their bulky bodies.

After making infuriated protests, most of the herd moved away, leaving small groups still undecided in the bush. We waited for them to follow and eventually all but two went off; these stood their ground and seemed to have no intention of budging.

George wanted to see the kill which had attracted the birds and since the light was failing he decided to walk, with Makedde, between the two remaining groups of elephant. Meanwhile, Ibrahim and I stood on the roof of the car and kept a close watch on the beasts, so that we could warn George of their movements. He found a freshly killed water buck and lion spoor around it. Very

49

little had been eaten, so plainly the lion had been interrupted by the arrival of the elephants.

As soon as we got to camp we fired a signal to Elsa but she failed to appear.

However, the next morning we found her and her cubs on the Big Rock. As soon as she spotted us she rushed down and ended by throwing the whole of her weight against George who was squashed by her affection, then she bowled me over, while the puzzled cubs craned their heads above the high grass to see what was going on.

When we got back to camp we provided a meal for them over which they competed with such growls, snarls and spankings that we thought they must be very hungry. Little Elsa had the best of it and eventually went off with her loot, leaving her brothers still so hungry that we felt obliged to produce another carcase for them.

Later, while we were resting, Jespah, with surprising boldness, started chewing at my sandals and poking at my toes. As his claws and teeth were already well developed I quickly tucked my feet under me. He seemed most disappointed, so I stretched my hand slowly towards him in a friendly gesture. He watched it attentively, then looked at me and walked off.

That evening Elsa took up her usual position on the roof of the Land-Rover, but the cubs instead of romping about flung themselves on the ground and never stirred. As it was the hour at which they were usually most energetic, we were surprised. During the night I heard Elsa talking to them in a low moan and also heard suckling noises. They must indeed have been hungry to need to be suckled after consuming two goats in twenty-four hours.

One evening when Elsa and her cubs were walking back with us, she and Jespah got in front of us while Gopa and Little Elsa stayed behind. This worried Jespah very much; he rushed to and fro trying to marshal his pride, until his mother stood still, between us and him, and allowed us to pass her, thus reuniting the family. Afterwards she rubbed our knees affectionately as though to thank us for having taken the hint.

50

The next morning I woke up to hear Elsa moaning to the cubs in a nearby thicket. Since their birth we had never used the wireless when they were in camp so as not to frighten them. But to-day George turned on the morning news. Elsa appeared at once, looked at the instrument, roared at it at full strength and went on doing so until we turned it off. Then she went back to the cubs. After a while George tuned in again, whereupon Elsa rushed back and repeated her roars until he switched off.

I patted her and spoke reassuringly to her in a low voice, but she was not satisfied till she had made a thorough search inside the tent. Then she went to her family. I had often been asked how Elsa reacted to different sounds and had flattered myself that I knew how to answer these questions, but this reaction of hers was unexpected; before her release, when she was living with us, we had listened daily to the wireless, and though when we first tuned in she had always been startled, as indeed she usually was if I played the piano, as soon as she realised where the sounds came from she paid no attention to them. She differentiated between the engine of a car and of a plane. However loud the noise of the plane might be she ignored it, but the faintest vibration from a car engine alerted her, often before we heard it. I had tried singing to her to test her reactions, but whatever the melody I never observed any response. On the other hand, when occasionally I imitated the cubs' call in order to make her search for them she reacted at once as I intended she should, but if I did this for fun she paid no attention.

As a wild animal she could of course recognise various animal sounds and interpret the mood of the approaching beast. She could also sense our mood by the intonation of our voices.

Lately we had had plenty of evidence that neighbouring tribesmen were trespassing, so we felt it would be a good thing if we could identify the lie-up Elsa was now most frequently using as this might enable us to come to her help if an emergency arose. We found it by what we called the Cave Rock. This contained a fine rainproof cavity with several 'platforms,' ideal resting places from which to survey the surrounding bush.

On 20th June the cubs were six months old; to celebrate their first half year George shot a guinea fowl. Little Elsa, of course, took possession of it and disappeared into the bush. Her indignant brothers went after her but returned defeated and tumbling down a sandy bank landed on their mother. She was lying on her back, her four paws straight up in the air. She caught the cubs and held their heads in her mouth. They struggled to free themselves and then pinched Mum's tail. After a splendid game together, Elsa got up and walked up to me in a dignified manner and embraced me gently as though to show that I was not to be left out in the cold. Jespah looked bewildered. What could he make of this? Here was his mother making such a fuss of me, so I couldn't be bad, but all the same I was so different from them. Whenever I turned my back on him, he stalked me, but each time I turned and faced him he stopped and rolled his head from side to side, as though he did not know what to do next. Then he seemed to find the solution; he would go off; he walked straight into the river evidently intending to cross to the other bank. Elsa rushed after him. I shouted, 'No, no,' but without effect and the rest of the family quickly followed them. Young as he was Jespah had now taken on the leadership of the pride and was accepted by the family.

When they returned Elsa dozed off with her head on my lap. This was too much for Jespah. He crept up and began to scratch my shins with his sharp claws. I could not move my legs because of the weight of Elsa's head resting on them, so in an effort to stop him I stretched my hand slowly towards him. In a flash he bit it and made a wound at the base of my forefinger. All this happened within a few inches of Elsa's face but she diplomatically ignored the incident and closed her eyes sleepily.

After this we all returned to camp and Jespah seemed so friendly that I began to wonder whether when he bit me it was only in play. Certainly, between himself and his mother, biting was a proof of affection.

By now we were, however, beginning to worry about his relationship to us. We had done our best to respect the cubs' natural instincts and not to do anything to prevent them from being wild lions, but inevitably this had resulted in our having no control over them. Little Elsa and her timid brother were as shy as ever and never provoked a situation which required chastisement. But Jespah had a very different character, and I could not push his sharp, scratching claws back by saying, 'No, no,' as I used to do when Elsa was a cub and so taught her to retract her claws when playing with us. On the other hand, I did not want to use a stick. Elsa might resent it if I did and indeed she might cease to trust me. Our only hope seemed to lie in establishing a friendly relationship with Jespah, but for the moment his variable reactions made a truce more possible than a friendship.

Several weeks later, George and I were to join up at the camp, as he had been out on patrol and I had been to Isiolo. As I approached the camp I was worried because I did not see George and drove on filled with foreboding which was increased when, as I drew nearer, the air became so full of smoke that my lungs were stinging.

When we arrived I could hardly believe my eyes. The thorn bushes were in ashes and smouldering tree trunks added to the grilling heat. The two acacia trees which provided shade and were the home of many birds were scorched. In the charred and blackened scene the green canvas of the tents stood out in sharp contrast. I was much relieved when I found George inside one of them eating his lunch.

He had plenty to tell me. When he had arrived, two days earlier, he found the camp burning and seen the footprints of twelve poachers. Not only had they set fire to the trees and the thorn enclosure but they had also destroyed everything they could find.

George had been very worried about Elsa and had fired several thunder flashes without getting any response. Then she and the cubs had suddenly appeared, all ravenously hungry. Within two hours they had eaten an entire goat. Elsa had been most affectionate and had several times come to lie on George's bed during the night: he noticed that she had several wounds. She left at dawn; soon afterwards he followed her spoor and eventually saw her sitting on the Whuffing Rock.

Then he went off to try and discover where she had come from

53

on the previous evening. Her spoor which led down from the river was mixed up with the footprints of the poachers. He wondered whether they had been hunting Elsa and the cubs.

After lunch he sent three Game Scouts to search for the camp burners. They returned with six of the culprits. He kept them busy rebuilding the camp, which was no agreeable task, considering the amount of thorny bush which they were obliged to cut for our enclosures.

Elsa and her cubs who had spent the night in camp left soon after daybreak. Half an hour later George heard roars coming from the direction of the Big Rock, which was the way they had gone, so he assumed it must be Elsa; he was therefore much astonished to hear her voice coming from across the river soon afterwards. Then she appeared wet and without the cubs and seemed very agitated: she had several bleeding marks on her hind-quarters.

In a few minutes she left hurriedly, rushing towards the Big Rock calling loudly. George felt sure that she must recently have had an encounter with an enemy for her wounds were not made by a quarry; also, her nervous state suggested that she knew that whatever beast had threatened her was still in the neighbourhood. George now thought that the roars he had first taken for Elsa's were probably those of some fierce lion who had attacked her and that while the two were fighting the cubs had scattered and after the battle Elsa had escaped across the river. Now he followed Elsa in search of her family.

Together they climbed up the Big Rock. When they got to its top Elsa called in a very worried tone of voice. Of the cubs there was no sign. George and Elsa searched back and forth between the rocks and the camp. Suddenly she became much interested in a patch of dense bush which she sniffed attentively and then called towards. George investigated it; he saw no sign of the cubs inside the thicket, but Elsa remained beside it while he went back to camp to collect Nuru to join in the search. All morning they looked for spoor but found only Elsa's pug marks.

After a long fruitless trek George sent Nuru back to camp and carried on alone until he found Elsa at the base of the Whuffing

Rock, still calling desperately for her children. Together they crept along the ridge, looking into all possible hideouts. They found the spoor of a large lion and of a lioness and Elsa seemed most upset. During the morning she had insisted on taking the lead, but now she was content to follow George.

When they reached the end of the rock, near to the place where the cubs were born, Elsa sniffed very persistently into a cleft. Suddenly George saw one cub peeping over the top of the rock above them and soon another appeared; they were Little Elsa and Gopa. Jespah was missing.

When they saw their mother they rushed down and rubbed noses with her and finally went off with her towards the 'kitchen lugga.' All this had taken place just before I had arrived and as soon as he had finished his lunch George intended to look for Jespah. Naturally I went with him.

After about an hour Elsa appeared at the foot of the Big Rock and gave me a most heartening welcome.

While all this was going on the cubs remained in the bush and Elsa paid no attention to them. To encourage them to come to their mother we retired behind some rocks and after a while they rushed to her.

As soon as they were safely settled on the top of the ridge, George went off to search for Jespah by the Zom rocks, while I investigated the foot of the range. After George returned, she and the two cubs joined us below the rock.

Now she trotted ahead of us towards the thicket which had interested her so much in the morning. Just after she had passed it I suddenly saw that not two, but three cubs were scampering behind Elsa, in the most casual manner. Jespah's reappearance after a day's absence seemed to be taken by the family as the most natural thing in the world. We, however were greatly relieved and followed them to the river where they stopped for a long drink, while we went ahead to prepare a carcase for them in camp. When finally we were able to sit down and enjoy our dinner we discussed Elsa's curious behaviour. Why had she not persevered in the search for Jespah? Had she known all the time that he was hiding in the thicket? But was this likely? Why should he have remained alone for twelve hours only a very short distance from the camp, the river and the rocks where the rest of his family were; and why had he not answered his mother's call and ours?

Had the strange lions still been near the rocks, this would have explained Elsa's fears and Jespah's, but had this been the case it was unlikely that the other two cubs would have chosen to take refuge there.

After dinner George had to start back for Isiolo to prepare for a three weeks' safari. Soon after he had left the lions began to roar from the Big Rock and kept on calling for most of the night. Elsa, when she heard them, at once moved herself and the cubs as near as possible to my enclosure and stayed there till dawn; then she took them across the river. Later I saw their pug marks on the sandbank just below the camp. They were mixed up with buffalo spoor; this beast remained near us for some time, did not seem to be troubled by our presence and came each night, just below the tents, to drink.

During these days I made some attempts to shoot crocodile but without much success.

Elsa and the cubs were well aware that the 'crocs' were not friendly and often watched the water attentively for any suspicious eddy or floating sticks. On the other hand, their reactions were inconsistent, and I was anxious about their safety.

One afternoon I called to Elsa, who was on the far bank. She appeared at once and was preparing to swim across with the cubs, when suddenly they all froze and stared intently into the water. Then Elsa took the cubs higher up the river and they appeared opposite the 'kitchen lugga.' Here the water is very shallow in the dry season. In spite of this they did not cross for an hour, nor did the cubs indulge in their usual splashing and ducking games. This was reassuring for it showed their prudence, but it was characteristic of their variable reactions that next day when I called Elsa from the same place at the same time, they all swam across at once, and without the slightest hesitation.

When it was getting dark we were all sitting near the river. Suddenly Elsa and the cubs looked at the water, stiffened and pulled grimaces and three or four yards away I saw a 'croc.' I knew that he must have been a big fellow for his head was about a foot long.

I fetched my rifle and killed him. Although the cubs were less than three feet from me, the shot did not upset them. Elsa afterwards came and rubbed her head against my knee as though to thank me.

Nearly every afternoon she brought her cubs to the sandbank. Among its attractions were fresh buffalo droppings and sometimes elephant balls as well; in these they rolled to their great satisfaction. The cubs also played on the fallen palm logs. There was no question, when they fell off as they frequently did, of their landing on their feet, like the proverbial cat; on the contrary they fell clumsily on to the grass like a dropped parcel and seemed most surprised at their abrupt descent.

It was about this time that Jespah became more friendly. Now he sometimes licked me and once even stood on his hind legs to embrace me. Elsa took great care not to show too much affection to me in the presence of the cubs, but when we were alone was as devoted as usual. Her trust in me was as complete as ever and she even allowed me to take her meat from her claws and move it to a more suitable spot when I thought this necessary. She also permitted me to handle the cubs' meat. For instance, in the evening when I wanted to remove a partly eaten carcase from the river-bank so that the 'crocs' should not finish it off, she never interfered, even if I was obliged to drag it over her, and, still more remarkable, even when the cubs were hanging on to it and defending it.

At dusk the cubs were always full of energy and played tricks on their mother which made it hard for her to retain her dignity. Jespah, for instance, discovered that when he stood on his hind legs and clasped her tail she could not easily free herself. In this fashion they would walk round in circles, Jespah behaving like a clown until Elsa had had enough of it and sat down on top of him. He seemed to be delighted by her way of putting an end to the game and would lick and hug his mother until she escaped into our tent.

But it was not long before the tent ceased to provide her with an asylum, for he followed her into it, giving a quick look round and then sweeping everything he could reach to the ground. During the night I often heard him busily engaged in sorting through the food boxes and the beer crate; the clattering bottles provided him with endless entertainment. He became quite at home in the tent, but his brother and sister were less venturesome. They stayed outside watching the fun.

7. ELSA'S FIGHT

One morning Makedde observed vultures circling and, going to the spot about a mile downstream, found the remains of a rhino which had been killed by poisoned arrows the day before while drinking.

The poachers had left plenty of footprints and had erected machans on trees close to the drinking place. They must have been well informed and known that I was alone with only Makedde to guard the place, for had George been with me, they would never have dared to indulge in these activities so close to the camp.

For three days Elsa arrived in camp long after dark, and on the fourth brought only two cubs; Jespah was missing. I was very worried, so after waiting for some time, I began repeating his name over and over again, till Elsa decided to go upstream and look for him, taking the two cubs with her.

For over an hour I heard her calling, till the sound gradually receded into the distance.

Then suddenly there were savage lion growls, accompanied by the terrified shrieks of baboons. As it was dark I could not go to see what was happening and awaited the outcome feeling miserable, for I was sure that Elsa was being attacked by lions.

She came back after a while, her head and shoulders covered with bleeding scratches and the root of her right ear bitten through. This was much the worst injury she had ever suffered. Little Elsa and Gopa came back with her and sat a short distance away looking very frightened.

I sat a long time with Elsa; she held her head on one side and the blood dripped from her wound. Eventually she rose, called the cubs and waded across the river.

I could hardly wait till it was light to go and look for Jespah.

Next morning, following Elsa's spoor, Makedde, Nuru and I went to the Cave Rock and were much relieved to find the family reunited. I was happy to know that Jespah was safe and that I could now concentrate on treating his mother. But Elsa was not co-operative and each time I approached her head she moved away, apparently with considerable effort. Suddenly I was startled to hear voices. I thought they were probably those of poachers. I had to think quickly. Was it best to stay put? Probably not, for Elsa did not seem to want our company and might well go off with the cubs and fall into the poacher's hands. I went back to camp, hoping that as she must be hungry she would follow.

I waited anxiously till the late afternoon for Elsa and her family to arrive for their evening meal. After Elsa had settled down for the night a lion began calling. This seemed to alarm her and she shortly afterwards went off with the cubs.

The next night I heard two lions grunting as they cracked the bones of the carcase which was lying in front of George's tent. They spent a long time over their meal and only went off at dawn when the boys began talking in the kitchen.

Elsa kept away for some days. I thought her absence was explained by the presence of this pair who had remained nearby, and who the following night grunted round the goat truck.

After Elsa had been absent for four days I became very anxious, for her wound must be a very big handicap to her in hunting, and I was afraid also that the poachers might do her some harm. When on the evening of the 20th July I saw vultures circling, my heart sank. We went to investigate but all we found was more evidence of the poachers. They had made hides near to every drinking place, on both sides of the river. We also found the ashes of recent fires and charred animal bones.

A week earlier when Makedde had found poisoned arrowheads in a rhino, I had sent a message to the Warden of the reserve, asking him to send Scouts to patrol the area. Now on our return to camp we found that they had arrived and I was very glad to see them. With our reinforcements we set out next morning to look for Elsa and arranged that if anyone spotted her they should fire a shot.

Three hours later I heard a report and returned to camp to be told by two of the newcomers that they had seen Elsa and the cubs under a bush on the opposite side of the river, about a mile inland.

She was lying in the shade and the cubs were asleep. She had seen the men approach but had not moved. This sounded odd, unless she were so ill that she did not care if even strangers were close by.

Makedde suggested that we should take some meat to her, but not enough to satisfy her hunger, and so tempt her to come back to camp. As we approached her lie-up I signalled to the men to stay behind and called to her.

She emerged, walking slowly, her head bent low to one side. I was surprised and alarmed that she should have settled in such an exposed place where she could easily be seen by poachers. She was obviously in great pain. Meanwhile, the cubs fought over the section of carcase we had brought them and soon there was nothing left for Elsa but polished bones. She looked on resignedly and certainly gave the lie to the well-established legend that lionesses gorge themselves and let their cubs go hungry. Jespah thanked me for his meal by licking my hand with his rough tongue. I tried to induce Elsa to come back to camp by calling, 'Magi, Chakulu, Nyama,' but as she did not move, I went home without her.

By now I had been three weeks alone in camp and George was overdue. In his absence wild lions prowled round the camp every night and although Makedde and Ibrahim could have used their rifles if an emergency arose, I was nervous about the safety of the boys.

At last George arrived and was greeted by the roars of a strange lion. Hearing that Elsa had not been seen for several days, he decided to go and look for her, and he was also determined to try to scare off the strange lion, and his fierce lioness who had so often injured Elsa. We knew her and her mate quite well by now; at least by voice, and we were also familar with their spoor. They ranged along the river for about ten miles. Of course they shared the country with other lions besides Elsa, but she was the only one who kept permanently to the vicinity of the camp. The fierce lioness had lived in this region long before Elsa but we did not know what she had done to displease this disagreeable beast. We were pretty sure that she had not competed for the attention of her mate, but had kept strictly to her own young lion. Perhaps Elsa had interfered with her hunting or her territorial claims, or perhaps the creature was just bad-tempered. Anyway, we were sure now that she had chased Elsa and the cubs over the river and towards the poachers and that she and her mate had, for several days, taken over the Big Rock.

We searched upstream on the far side of the river. Here there were plenty of lion pug marks – including those of a lioness with three cubs. They led us five miles from camp to a part of the bush which, so far as we knew, Elsa had never visited. As we approached a baobab tree, we heard the sound of startled animals bolting and the Toto caught a glimpse of the hindquarters of a lion and of three cubs which could have been Elsa's. They were gone in a flash and though we called and called there was no response.

George and I followed their tracks for some way, but we were puzzled; if they were Elsa's family why had they rushed away from us? On the other hand, was it likely that there was another lioness about with three cubs of around the same size as Elsa's? On our way back we found fresh spoor of a lion leading in the direction we had just come from.

We spent the next two days covering the boundaries of Elsa's territory, partly on foot and partly by car. We searched on an average for eight hours a day. We learned nothing of Elsa, but a lot about the poachers. We destroyed many of their hides and in one found a bit of rope which I had used to fasten the wicker gate of my tent enclosure.

George left in the last week of July and I continued to search for Elsa. The next morning, walking with Makedde along the car track towards the Big Rock, we traced the spoor of a single lion who had evidently come towards the camp; I saw also the imprints of pointed shoes. Both spoors were superimposed on the tyre marks of George's car.

Plainly the poachers were keeping an eye on our movements and no doubt, having heard George's car go off, had next morning come to reconnoitre. How disappointed they must have been to discover that I was still in residence.

It was very hot and, after several hours of tracking, Makedde and I sat down to rest.

My spirits were very low. It was now over a fortnight since the fierce lioness had attacked Elsa and except for the occasion when the Game Scout had found her in the bush, she had not been seen, nor had there been any trace of the cubs. I was particularly worried because, during the time in which I had observed Elsa's wounds, instead of healing, their condition had grown worse. In such a state, could she, I wondered, hunt and provide food for herself and for the cubs? Also, the presence of the poachers provided another and perhaps even more serious cause for anxiety.

Feeling miserable, I asked Makedde whether he loved Elsa. He looked startled but replied warmly: 'Where is she that I could love her?' This made me even more depressed. Makedde, watching me, scolded more angrily: 'You have nothing but death in your mind, you think of death, you speak of death and you behave as though there were no Mungo (God) who looks after everything. Can't you trust him to look after Elsa?'

On the evening of the sixteenth day since Elsa and the cubs had disappeared, after lighting the lamps I poured myself a drink and sat in the dark straining my ears for any hopeful sound. Then, suddenly, there was a swift movement, and I was nearly knocked off my chair by Elsa's affectionate greeting. She looked thin but fit and the wound in her ear was healing. Plainly she was very hungry for when the boys came towards us with the carcase I had asked for, she rushed at them. I yelled, 'No, Elsa, no.' She stopped, obediently returned to me and controlled herself until the meat had been attached to a chain in front of the tent, then she pounced on it and ate voraciously. She seemed to be in a great hurry, gorged herself on half the goat and then withdrew out of the lamplight and cunningly moved farther away till she finally disappeared in the direction of the studio.

I was immensely relieved to know that she was well, but where were the cubs? Her visit had only lasted half an hour and I waited long into the night hoping that she might return with them to finish off the goat.

At dawn on the 1st August I was woken by the miaowing of the cubs and saw them crawling close to my thorn enclosure. I called to the boys to bring the meat and joined Elsa who was watching her youngsters fighting over the meat.

The cubs growled, snarled and cuffed at each other for the best bits of meat. Living in the bush had certainly made them become more wild, for now they were constantly on the alert for suspicious sounds and nearly panicked when some baboons barked.

The two little cubs were shyer than ever and were frightened if I made the least movement, but, to my surprise, Jespah came up to me, tilted his head on one side with a questioning look, licked my arm and plainly wished to remain friends.

The sun was high, it was getting hot, and so when the cubs had eaten all they could they had a splendid game in the shallows, ducking, wrestling, splashing and churning up the water till at last they collapsed in the shade on a rock, where Elsa joined them.

As I watched them dozing contentedly with their paws dangling over the boulder I humbly remembered Makedde's reprimand for my lack of faith – a happier family one could not wish to see.

8. EXCITEMENTS OF THE BUSH

At about nine that evening Elsa and the cubs came from the river and settled themselves in front of my tent and demanded their supper. As the remains of the meat was still by the gardenia bush I call to Makedde and the Toto and asked them to come and help me drag it in. I collected a pressure lamp and we went down the narrow path which we had cut through the dense bush from the camp to the river.

Makedde, armed with a stick and a hurricane-lamp, went ahead, the Toto followed close behind, and carrying my bright light I brought up the rear. Silently we walked a few yards down the path. Then there was a terrific crash, out went Makedde's lamp and a second later mine was smashed as a monstrous black mass hit me and knocked me over.

The next thing I knew was that Elsa was licking me. As soon as I could collect myself I sat up and called to the boys. A feeble groan came from the Toto who was lying close to me holding his head, then he got up shakily, stammering, 'Buffalo, buffalo.' At this moment we heard Makedde's voice coming from the direction of the kitchen; he was yelling that he was all right. As we pulled ourselves together the Toto told me that he had seen Makedde suddenly jump to the side of the path and hit out with his stick at a buffalo. The next moment the Toto had been knocked over and then I had been overrun. What had happened when Elsa and the buffalo met face to face none of us will ever know. Luckily the Toto had no worse injury than a bump on his head. I felt blood running down my arms and thighs and was in some pain, but I wanted to get home before examining my wounds. This incident certainly belied the popular belief that a lion however tame becomes savage at the scent or taste of blood.

Elsa, who had obviously come to protect us from the buffalo, seemed to realise that we were hurt and was most gentle and affectionate.

I was worried about Makedde and went at once to the kitchen to see what condition he was in. There I found him, unhurt and having a splendid time, recounting to his awestruck friends his single-handed combat with the buffalo. I am afraid his heroic stature was slightly diminished by the appearance of my bleeding legs, but the main thing was that we were all safe.

One evening when Nuru was herding the goats towards my truck, Jespah made a beeline for them, rushed through the kitchen, passed within a few inches of the devout Ibrahim, who was kneeling on his mat absorbed in his evening prayers, dodged between the water containers and round the open fire and arrived at the truck just as the goats were about to enter it.

There was no doubt as to his intentions, so I ran and grabbed a stick, and holding it in front of him shouted, 'No, no,' in my most commanding voice.

Jespah looked puzzled, sniffed the stick and began spanking it playfully, which gave Nuru time to lift the goats into the truck. Then Jespah walked back with me to Elsa who had been watching the game. Often she helped me to control him, either by adding a cuffing to my 'noes' or by placing herself between the two of us. But I wondered how long it would be before, even with her support, my commands and my sticks failed to have any effect. Jespah was so full of life and curiosity and fun; he was a grand little wild lion, and a very fast-growing one too, and it was high time that we left him and his brother and sister to live a natural life. While I was thinking this, he was chasing after the other cubs, and in doing so tipped the water bowl over Elsa giving her a drenching. He got a clout for his pains and then she squashed him under her heavy, dripping body. It was a funny sight and we laughed but this was tactless and offended Elsa, who, after giving us a disapproving look, walked off followed by her two well-behaved cubs.

One evening Elsa came in very late and settled near the tents while Jespah, who was in one of his energetic moods, amused himself upsetting everything within reach; the tables were swished clear of bottles, plates and cutlery, the rifles were pulled out of their stands and the haversacks full of ammunition carried away, and cardboard containers were first proudly paraded in front of the other cubs and then torn to shreds. In the morning we found the family still in camp, a most unusual occurrence. The boys kept well inside the kitchen fence waiting for them to go, then, as they showed no intention of leaving, George walked up to Elsa, whereupon she knocked him down. After this George released me from my thorn enclosure and I tried my luck. I approached Elsa, called to her, but as she looked at me through half-closed eyes, I kept on my guard while she came slowly towards me, and I was justified, for when she was within ten yards of me she charged at full speed, knocked me down, sat on me and then proceeded to lick me.

She was extremely friendly, so this, it seemed, was no more than her idea of a morning game. But she knew quite well that the knocking-down trick was not popular with us and this was the first time since the birth of the cubs that she had indulged in it.

Later she took the cubs to a place below the studio, and in the afternoon we joined them there. Jespah was very much interested in George's rifle and tried his best to snatch it away from him, but soon he realised that it was impossible to do this so long as its owner was on his guard; after this discovery it was amusing to see how he tried to distract George's attention by pretending to chase his brother and sister. When George's suspicions were allayed and he put the rifle down to pick up his camera, Jespah pounced on it and straddled it. A real tug-of-war followed, which Elsa watched attentively. Finally, she came to George's rescue by sitting on her son and thereby forcing him to release his hold on the gun.

Poor Jespah, he still had a lot to learn, not about the wild life which is his, but about the strange world which is ours and which he showed so great a wish to investigate. One night, for instance, I heard him apparently very 'busy' in George's tent. How 'busy' I only discovered next morning when I noticed that my field-glasses were missing. Eventually, I found bits of their leather case in the bush below the tent. They bore the imprint of Jespah's milk teeth. Close by lay the glasses, and luckily, by some miracle, the lenses were intact. Yes, there was no doubt that Jespah could be a nuisance but he was irresistible and one couldn't be cross with him for long.

At eight months he had now lost his baby fluff but his coat was as soft as a rabbit's. He had begun to imitate his mother and to wish to be treated by us as she was. Sometimes he would come and lie under my hand, evidently expecting to be patted and, though it was against my principles, I occasionally did so. He often wanted to play with me, but though his intentions were entirely friendly I never felt sure that he might not bite or scratch me as he would his own family. He was not like Elsa who controlled her strength on such occasions, for he was much closer to a wild lion.

We were both very interested in observing the different relationships which Elsa's cubs were developing towards us. Jespah, prompted by an insatiable curiosity, had overcome his earlier inhibitions, mixed with us and was most friendly, but allowed no familiarities.

Little Elsa was truly wild, snarled if we came close and then sneaked away. Though she was less boisterous than her brothers, she had a quiet and efficient way of getting what she wanted. Once I watched Jespah trying to drag a freshly killed goat into a bush. He pulled and tugged and somersaulted across it – but nothing would move the carcase. Then Gopa came to his aid and between the two they tried their best – but finally gave up exhausted and sat panting next to it. Now Little Elsa, who had watched their exertions, came along and pulling hard, straddled the heavy load into a safe place where she was joined at once by her panting brothers.

Gopa quite often made use of the tent when the tsetse were most active, and it was on these occasions that I noticed how jealous he was. For instance, if I sat near Elsa he would look long and scrutinisingly into my eyes with an expression of disapproval and made it extremely plain that she was his 'Mum' and that he would prefer me to leave her alone. One evening I was sitting at the entrance of the tent while he was in the annexe at the far end and Elsa lay between us watching both of us. When Gopa started chewing at the tent-canvas, I said as firmly as I could, 'No, no', to my surprise, he snarled at me, but stopped chewing. A little later he took up the canvas again and, though my 'No' was answered with another snarl, he again stopped.

So far, all the cubs responded when we said 'No' although we had never enforced our prohibition with a stick or anything else which could frighten them.

By the beginning of September the drought was severe. Thanks to patrolling by the anti-poaching team which George had called in, few wild animals had been killed, but the team could not remain indefinitely in the area, since their services were urgently required in other parts of the country. When they left George would only have his small staff to depend on and there was no hope of the rains beginning till the end of October.

It was welcome news when we heard that Sir Julian Huxley was soon coming on a mission sponsored by UNESCO to investigate the problem of the conservation of wild life in East Africa. When he wrote asking us if we could show him parts of the Northern Frontier Province we were very pleased as this would give us the opportunity of acquainting him with the local problems, and the lack of means for dealing with them.

We believed that Sir Julian's visit would be a great encouragement to all those interested in the preservation of wild life. We also knew that he wished to see Elsa. We limited her visitors to those who had good and sufficient reasons for seeing her and, as Sir Julian clearly had those, we were glad that he should spare time to do so.

Late one afternoon we arrived in Elsa's domain with Sir Julian.

We fired the usual signal shots and twenty minutes later were delighted to hear the barking of baboons which usually heralded the arrival of Elsa and the cubs. In her enthusiastic welcome she nearly knocked me down and then hopped on to the top of the Land-Rover. Meanwhile, the cubs were busy dragging the carcase we had provided for them into a 'safe' place. For half an hour we watched them and then left. Elsa had a very puzzled expression when she saw the cars going off after such a short visit.

After we had returned to camp George arrived bringing a lorry as well as his car, and, attracted by the noise of the engines, Elsa and the cubs soon turned up. George told me that next morning David Attenborough and Jeff Mulligan were arriving from London and that we were to collect them at the nearest airstrip. For some time we had been corresponding with David Attenborough about making a film of Elsa and her cubs for the B.B.C.

We had had previous suggestions for filming her but these we had refused fearing that the arrival of a large film unit might upset her. The coming of only two people was much less worrying, but even they would need constant protection. We hoped to provide for their safety at night by making one sleep in my lion-proof Land-Rover which was driven into a large thorn enclosure; our other guest's sleeping quarters were to be a tent rigged up on a lorry which also stood in the enclosure.

Soon after we had gone to bed we heard a lion roaring upstream and observed that Elsa at once left the camp. Next morning, the 13th September, George called me early to his tent and there I saw Elsa, in a terrible state, her head, chest, shoulders and paws covered with deep bleeding gashes. She appeared to be very weak and when I knelt beside her to examine her wounds, she only looked at me. We were very much surprised for we had not heard any growls during the night and were quite unaware that a fight had taken place. When I began to try to dress her wounds Elsa struggled to her feet and slowly dragged herself towards the river, obviously in great pain. It was the worst moment to have visitors – let alone film producers, and I feared that they might have no chance of doing any work. I greeted them with this depressing news and soon realised that we had been more than lucky in finding two such animal lovers as David and Jeff.

We arrived in camp at lunch-time and found George who had just returned from a fruitless search for the cubs. While our guests settled in I went to look for Elsa and found her under a thick bush near the studio. She was breathing very fast and lay quite still as I swished the flies off her wounds.

Poor Elsa, I had never before seen her in so much pain. She made no effort to raise her head and it was only when I lifted it that she began to drink; then she lapped for a long time. After that she ate the meat but made it very plain that she did not want company, so we left ther.

Since there was nothing more we could do for Elsa, George and I set out to look for the cubs on the other side of the river. We walked shouting all the names by which we address Elsa and also calling Jespah. Finally, behind a bush, we caught sight of one cub, but as we approached it bolted. In order not to frighten it further we decided to go home and hope that the cubs would make their own way back to their mother. Jespah was the first to do so; about six in the evening he crossed the river and rushed up to Elsa, then we heard another cub miaowing from the far bank. Elsa heard it too, and dragged herself to the river-bank and began calling to it. It was Gopa and when he saw his mother he swam across. I provided some meat which the little lions devoured, but Elsa would not touch it. While Jespah and Gopa were eating we took our guests for a stroll along the river and were much surprised on our return to find Elsa on the roof of the Land-Rover which was parked in front of our tents. We had our drinks and our supper within a few yards of her, but she took no notice of us. We remained anxious about Little Elsa until some time after we had gone to bed George spotted her coming into the camp.

Soon after midnight the family moved off and a little later we heard the roars of the fierce lioness. During the following day Elsa kept away, and we knew why, for George saw the fierce lioness on the Big Rock. That night we again heard her roaring. We were very worried about Elsa, so, as soon as it was light, George went upriver to try to find her, while I went in the opposite direction accompanied by Makedde, Nuru and a Game Scout; we carried water with us in case we found her. We picked up Elsa's spoor half a mile beyond the Border Rock, which was farther than we had ever known her to go. I began calling and presently she came out from behind some rocks. She reconnoitred the neighbourhood to see whether all was safe and then the cubs appeared. They were terribly thirsty. I could not pour the water out quickly enough and I had some difficulty in avoiding getting scratched and in preventing the plastic water bowl from being torn out of my hands.

When we started for home and rejoined the boys who had stayed behind, both Elsa and Jespah sniffed very suspiciously at the Game Scout. He followed my advice and stood absolutely rigid but his face betrayed less ease than his action suggested. As soon as it was possible I sent him ahead to camp with Makedde.

Elsa's wounds had improved but still needed dressing. It took a lot of coaxing to get the family to follow us and we made our way slowly back to camp. Nuru stayed with me as gun-bearer, but when I thought we were nearly home I told him to go on and warn David of our coming, so that he would be able to film the lions crossing the river. After he had gone I felt a little uneasy and then became really worried for I found that I had miscalculated the distance and had lost myself in the bush. By then it was midday and very hot and the lions stopped under every bush to pant in the shade. I knew that the best thing to do was to find the nearest lugga and follow it, for it must lead to the river from which I would be able to get my bearings. Fairly soon I came upon a narrow lugga and walked along between its steep banks. Elsa followed me and the cubs scampered along some way behind her. I had turned a bend when I suddenly found myself standing face to face with a rhino. There was no question of 'jumping nimbly aside and allowing the charging beasts to pass' as one is supposed to do in such encounters, so I turned and ran back along my tracks just as fast as I could with the snorting creature puffing behind me. At last I saw a little gap in the bank and before I knew I had done it, I was up it and running into the bush. At this moment the rhino must have seen Elsa for it swerved abruptly, turned round and crashed up the opposite side. Elsa stood very still watching the pair of us. This was very lucky for me and I was extremely glad that she had not followed her usual habit of chasing any rhino she saw.

A few moments later I was greatly relieved to see Nuru coming towards me. I was going to thank him for running to my rescue, but before I had time to speak he told me that he, too, had met a rhino and been chased by it and that this was what had brought him to where I was. We had a good laugh over our frights and then, keeping close together, we went back to the camp.

Assuming that there would be no opportunity of filming the lions till late the next day we spent the morning photographing hyrax on the rocks. We returned hot and exhausted to a belated lunch and then went down to the studio, where camp beds had been put out for us so that we could enjoy a siesta. The beds were set out in a row, mine was on the outside, David's in the middle and George's beyond his. Jeff was some way off loading the cameras. Soon I fell asleep but woke up very suddenly to find a wet Elsa sitting on top of me, licking me affectionately and keeping me a prisoner under her immense weight; simultaneously David took a leap over George and went to join Jeff. Between them they quickly got the cameras working. Elsa made a bound on to George, greeted him affectionately and then walked in a most dignified manner up to the tents and settled herself inside one of them. She completely ignored the presence of our guests and behaved in the same way later in the evening when we were having our drinks.

Next morning we followed her spoor and found her half-way up the Whuffing Rock sleeping. As we did not wish to disturb her, we went home and only came back after tea. This time we took with us a sufficient number of cameras to take films from every angle.

We were very lucky for she and the cubs could not have been more obliging and posed beautifully on the saddle of the rock. Finally, Elsa came down and this time she greeted all of us, including David and Jeff, by rubbing her head gently against our knees. She stayed with us until it got dark and we went back to camp, but the cubs, possibly made nervous by the presence of strangers, stayed on the rock.

Although Elsa had not seemed upset by being filmed I wondered whether she would come for her evening meal. Lately if even one of her favourite boys was visible she had kept away from the camp. I need not have worried; just as I was going to explain to our guests that she might very well not turn up I was nearly knocked over by her stormy greeting. The fact that she appeared confirmed my impression that while she has become much more nervous of Africans she does not seem in the least suspicious of Europeans.

I mixed a dish of her favourite meat with some cod liver oil and was taking it to her when Jespah ambushed me and licked the dish.

While this was happening Jeff was testing the sound recorder and happened to run through some recordings of the fierce lioness roaring. Jespah cocked his ears and tilted his head sideways as he listened attentively to the hated voice. Then he left his titbits and rushed to warn his mother of the danger.

On the following afternoon we again filmed Elsa on the rock and had further proof of her friendliness towards David and Jeff: this time she brought the cubs to play with us. I was most interested to observe that Jespah reacted just as Elsa used to when she was a cub; he knew at once whether someone liked him, felt a bit nervous of him or was really frightened, and treated him accordingly. David, I am sorry to say, was singled out for stalking and ambushing, and most of his time was spent trying to dodge Jespah.

9. RETURN TO THE WILD

During the second week of October, George returned to camp and for several days life went on uneventfully until one night the fierce lioness and her mate announced their arrival by impressive roarings from the Big Rock. Elsa took the hint and at once moved her family across the river.

Early next morning George saw the fierce lioness standing on the Big Rock clearly outlined against the sky. She allowed him to come within four hundred yards of her and then made off.

Elsa came in for a quick meal that evening but did not reappear for forty-eight hours. During this time we changed guard. Worried by Elsa's absence, I went out to look for her but could find no pug marks. Next morning we found her spoor and those of the cubs all over the camp, and I thought it very strange that they had made no sound to indicate their presence. Following the pug marks we found them mixed up with the imprints of rhino and elephant.

That evening the family turned up, but Elsa was in a queer mood; she showed no interest in me or in Gopa or Little Elsa and was entirely absrobed in Jespah. I felt really sorry for Gopa who tried very hard to attract her attention, rolling invitingly on his back with outstretched paws whenever his mother passed close to him, with no result except that she stepped over him to join Jespah.

About 8.30 p.m. two lions started roaring; all the family listened intently, but only Elsa and Jespah trotted quickly towards the studio; Gopa and Little Elsa after going a short way with them came back to finish their meal. They went on gorging until there was a frightening roaring so close that they rushed at full speed after their mother who by now had crossed the river.

I brought the remains of their meal into safety, which was as well, for the lion duet went on all through the night. The following afternoon when the light was already fading Makedde and I saw a lioness climbing up the Big Rock and then sitting on top of it – undoubtedly this was the fierce lioness. I got out my field-glasses and had my first look at her. She was much darker and heavier than Elsa and rather ugly. I observed that she was staring at us. Suddenly there was a scream close to us and the next moment the bush seemed to be alive with elephants. Makedde and I ran back to camp as fast as we could. All that evening the elephants trumpeted and rumbled as they went down to the river to drink. Besides this the lioness kept on roaring from the top of the rock. There was no question of sleep that night and Elsa naturally kept away.

In the morning we tracked the fierce lioness's pug marks and those of her mate; they had gone upstream back to the area in which we believed they usually lived. Elsa no doubt knew this for that night she brought the family into camp for their dinner. She now paid little attention to me until the cubs had settled down to their meal, then she was as affectionate as ever. This was plainly a new stratagem she had devised so as not to arouse their jealousy.

The air was oppressive and lightning streaked the horizon at frequent intervals; soon after I had gone to bed a strong wind started blowing, the trees creaked and the canvas of the tent flapped; then the first drops of rain fell and it was not long before I seemed to be under a water spout. The downpour continued throughout the night. We had not expected this deluge and had not hammered our tent pegs in; as a result the poles collapsed and I spent my time trying to raise them sufficiently to keep some shelter over my head, while a river seemed to run round my feet.

When at last the freezing hours came to an end with daybreak, I looked forward to a cup of hot tea to warm me up but none appeared, for the firewood was too wet to kindle and besides, the boys had spent the night in the same conditions as myself.

When I emerged I saw that George's tent had also collapsed and from inside it I heard Elsa moaning in a low voice. Soon she appeared with Jespah and Gopa, rather bedraggled but dry. But even this downpour had not induced Little Elsa to seek shelter and when I caught sight of her outside the thorn fence I saw that she was drenched.

I began to sort out our soaked belongings and remove them to the cars to save them from the lions, and in this I was 'helped' by Jespah who had great fun defending each box I wanted to move. When I had finished my work Elsa, Jespah, Gopa and I crowded into my tent and Little Elsa consented to come inside the flaps but no farther; at least she had some protection there.

The rain continued for four days with only short respites in the late afternoons; visibility was reduced to a few yards. This was nothing unusual, for the rains vary a great deal in this part of Kenya.

Within three days the scorched, parched surroundings of the camp had become green and the dry, brittle bush had turned into luxurious vegetation. But it seemed as though it had exhausted its strength in putting out such a profusion of many-coloured flowers, for within three or four days the ground was carpeted with many-coloured petals.

George had reached camp as soon as the condition of the ground made it possible for him to travel, and had brought five Game Scouts with him. They were to provide a permanent patrol and put down poaching. It was necessary that they should live some distance away from Elsa and from our camp, and so George now began supervising the establishment of their post and cutting a motor track to it.

In two weeks' time we hoped that this work would be well advanced, then we would start deserting Elsa for increasingly long periods so as to compel the cubs to go hunting with her and assume their true wild life. Our unexpectedly prolonged stay in the bush had caused them to get a little too used to camp life, and, though we had no control over them, Jespah was now on quite intimate terms with us; but apart from this their wild instincts were intact and certainly Gopa and Little Elsa only put up with us because they saw that their mother insisted that we were friends.

We wondered whether she communicated her wish that they

should not hurt us, which they were now well equipped to do, or whether they simply followed her example. Jespah in particular, when he was playing with us or when he was jealous, could have done a lot of damage if he had not controlled himself, but he always did so and even when he was in a temper gave us good warning of the fact.

Gopa was less friendly but so long as we left him alone did nothing to provoke an incident.

Little Elsa remained shy, though she now seemed less nervous of us than she used to be. We were surprised that none of the cubs ever attempted to follow Elsa on to the roof of the Land-Rover, though they often gazed up at their mother with disappointed expressions, when she was resting on the canvas to escape their teasing. Judging by their ability to climb trees they could very easily have jumped on to the bonnet and then taken another leap on to the roof, and indeed Elsa had done this at a younger age, but for some reason they seemed to regard the Land-Rover as out of bounds.

During George's absence Jespah and Gopa used his tent as a sort of 'den.' As a result on his return he found it rather crowded at night. I was a little worried; George prefers to sleep on a low bed and with Elsa, Jespah and Gopa around it I wondered whether one night there might not be trouble, but they behaved remarkably well. Whenever Jespah tried to play with his toes, George's authoritative 'no' made him stop at once.

The extent to which they felt at home was illustrated when one night Elsa rolled round and tipped over George's bed, throwing him on top of Jespah. No commotion followed and Gopa who was sleeping near George's head did not even move.

On another night when the family were sleeping in the tent a lion started calling from the far bank and Elsa at once took the family off. We wondered whether it might have been the fierce lioness, for next evening they dragged their dinner between the tent ropes and the outer fly, ate it and finally buried the stomach there, which was not very pleasant for George. Soon afterwards we heard roars and Elsa crossed the river with the cubs. The water was still very deep but next morning we found the explanation of their daring swim when we saw the pug marks of a single lioness close to the camp.

A day later when we were returning to camp we found the family except for Jespah gorging on a carcase. It was not long before we discovered the missing cub behind the tents enjoying a roast guinea fowl which he had stolen off the table, but he had such a mischievous expression that we could do nothing but laugh at the little rascal. We were surprised, however, that he preferred cooked meat to fresh.

We now noticed the first signs of adolescence in Jespah and Gopa; they had grown fine fluff round their faces and necks, and if they looked a bit unshaven their appearance was certainly very endearing.

That night a lion roared and when we later traced his pug marks they led to the Big Rock; evidently something had given the cubs a fright, for when Elsa swam over, they refused to follow her and she had to go back twice to encourage them before they, too, swam across. Once landed they had a great game, Elsa rolling Jespah round and round like a bundle, which he loved, and poor Gopa jumping clumsily between them asking to be noticed; when I came close to photograph them Gopa growled at me, whereupon Jespah gave him such a clout that he looked quite stupefied by his punishment. It was all done in fun, but it showed up the different characters of the brothers. But as always when they settled down to their dinner all jealousy was forgotten.

George had shot a guinea fowl and I brought it out hidden behind my back because I wanted to give it to Little Elsa. I waited for a moment in which only she was looking up and then showed it to her. She took in the situation at once and while continuing to eat with her brothers watched me carefully as I walked a little distance away. I waited until Jespah and Gopa were concentrating upon the meat and when only Little Elsa saw what I was doing, dropped the bird behind a bush. Then, when she alone was watching me, I kept on pointing from her to the guinea fowl until suddenly she rushed like a streak of lightning, seized the bird and took it into a thicket where she could eat it unmolested by the others.

Next day we saw the family sitting on the rocky platform on the opposite side of the river to the studio, below which there is a deep pool which was at one time inhabited by a large crocodile. The cubs seemed nervous and only Elsa swam across. We had brought a carcase with us, she grabbed it, and crossed the river with it, but this time avoided the pool and swam higher upstream where the bank was much steeper but where we had never seen 'crocs.'

The family were not apparently hungry, for they did not eat but indulged in a game of tree climbing; the cubs balanced on the sloping branches which overhung the river and seemed intent on tripping one another up and throwing their adversary into the water. Finally, Elsa joined them; she seemed to us to be giving them a demonstration of how to turn on a branch and how to go from one branch to another.

When it grew dark the meat was still untouched and as we neither wished to lose it nor to provoke a fight between Elsa and some chance predator George determined to recover it.

The first thing was to get the family over to our side, otherwise they would object to the removal of their 'kill.' While George went up the river out of their sight and began to wade across, I swung a guinea fowl temptingly in the air. This did the trick and brought the lions over to join me. Unfortunately, when George reached the carcase Elsa observed this, swam hurriedly back and defended it. It took a lot of coaxing on his part to let her allow him to float the 'kill' over, and even then she swam beside him with a very suspicious expression on her face. While this was going on the cubs rushed up and down the bank, obviously most upset but making no attempt to join Elsa. I was surprised for usually they showed no fear of the river and by now it was quite fordable.

Jespah in his playful moods liked acting the clown. One day when he was being especially lively, teasing everybody and asking for a game, I placed a round wooden tea tray in a branch that hangs over the river to see what he would do about it. He climbed up and tried to grip the inch-thick rim between his teeth, using one paw to steady it as it swayed. When he got a sufficiently good grip to carry it horizontally he came down very cautiously, pausing several times to make sure that we were watching him. Finally, he reached the ground and then paraded round with his trophy, until Little Elsa and Gopa chased him and put an end to his performance.

George's leave was coming to an end and this seemed to be the right time for us leave the camp. Elsa had by now got the upper hand of the fierce lioness and was able to defend her territory; the poachers seemed to have left the district and we hoped that they would not return at least until the next drought, by which time the Game Scouts would be able to deal with them, as their post was nearly completed and their patrols were already in action along the river.

Besides, the cubs were now powerful young lions, and it was time that they should hunt with their mother and live their natural life; also as they were growing increasingly jealous we considered that it would be unfair to provoke them by our affection for their mother into doing something which might be harmful.

We decided to space our absences. On the first occasion we had intended to leave for only six days, but in fact, because of very heavy rains, it was nine before I could return. I came alone and greatly missed George's help when I found myself obliged to dig the lorry and the Land-Rover out of the bog, a task that occupied us for two days.

Elsa did not turn up in answer to the shots we fired, nor were there any signs of spoor around the camp, but these might well have been washed away by the flooding of the river. After a while, I walked towards the Big Rock and came upon Elsa trotting along with the cubs; they were panting and had probably come a long way in answer to my signal. They were delighted to see me and Jespah struggled to get between Elsa and myself so as to receive his share of the welcome. Gopa and Little Elsa, however, kept their distance. All were in excellent condition and as fat as they had been when we left. Elsa had a few bites on her chin and neck but nothing serious. Gopa had grown a much longer and darker mane than Jespah, whose colouring was very

81

light in comparison to his brother's. In a year's time, I thought, what a handsome pride they would make, with two slender graceful lionesses, accompanied by one blond and one dark lion.

I had brought a carcase, but though Elsa settled down to it the cubs were in no hurry to eat and played about for some time before joining her. When she had had her fill she came over to me and was very affectionate and as the cubs were too busy eating to notice this there were no demonstrations of jealousy, which seemed to be what their mother had intended.

How anxious Elsa was to prevent rows or ill-feeling was clearly shown next day. I had given the cubs a guinea fowl and was watching them fighting over it. Gopa growled most alarmingly at Jespah, Little Elsa and myself. Hearing this, Elsa instantly rushed up to see what was going on, but as soon as she had satisfied herself that nothing serious had provoked Gopa, she returned to the roof of the Land-Rover.

A few minutes later, while the cubs were still eating, I went up to her; she snarled at me and spanked me twice. I retired immediately, surprised, as I did not think I had deserved such treatment. Soon afterwards Elsa jumped off the car and rubbed herself affectionately against me, obviously wishing to make up for her bad behaviour. I stroked her and she settled down beside me, keeping one paw against me. When the cubs joined us she rolled on to the other side and I ceased to exist for her.

She constantly showed how anxious she was for the cubs to be friends with us. One evening, after having gorged himself on the meat we had provided, Jespah came into the tent. He was too full to play and rolled on to his back because his bulging belly was more comfortable in that position. He looked at me plainly demanding to be patted. As he was in a docile mood I felt comparatively safe from his swiping paws and sharp claws, so I stroked his silky fur. He closed his eyes and made a sucking noise, a sure sign of contentment. Elsa, who had been watching us from the roof of the car, joined us and licked both Jespah and me, showing how glad she was to see us on such good terms.

This happy scene was abruptly ended by Gopa who sneaked up and sat on top of Elsa, with a most possessive expression which left me in no doubt that I was not wanted. So I withdrew a short distance and sketched the lions.

Fond as Elsa was of her children she never failed to discipline them when they were doing something of which she knew we disapproved, even when they were acting only in accordance with their natural instincts.

We usually kept the goats locked up inside my truck at night, but for a short time we were obliged to secure them inside a strong thorn enclosure because the truck had to go away for repairs. During this time, Jespah on one occasion besieged the boma so persistently that we were worried for the safety of the goats. All the tricks we invented to divert his attention failed to produce any effect. Then Elsa came to our aid. She pranced round her son trying to entice him away, but he paid no attention to her; then she spanked him repeatedly. He spanked back. It was amusing to watch the two outwitting each other. Finally, Jespah forgot all about the goats and followed Elsa into the tent where their dinner was waiting for them.

But when he had finished his meal Jespah, having been cheated of his fun with the goats, looked for other amusement.

He found a tin of milk which he rolled across the groundsheet of the tent until it was covered with a sticky mess. Then he took George's pillow, but the feathers tickled him, so he looked for another toy and, before I could stop him, seized a needle case which I was using and raced out into the dark with it. I was terrified that it would open under the pressure of his jaws and that he might swallow its contents, so I grabbed our supper, a roast guinea fowl, and ran after him. Luckily, the sight of the bird proved too much for him; he dropped the case, scattering the needles, pins, razor blades and scissors over the grass. We carefully collected them so they should not prove a danger to the cubs.

10. A NEW YEAR BEGINS

It was now time for us to go back to Isiolo and leave the cubs to a spell of wild life.

On the 3rd December I called on the District Commissioner in whose area Elsa's home lies. I wanted to give him the latest news of the cubs and to ask his advice as to how I could best use some of the royalties of *Born Free* to help to develop the Game Reserve in which she was living.

Elsa was an asset to the reserve because her story had aroused world-wide sympathy and understanding for wild life and also because part of the money I had received for her book had contributed to the sum needed to establish the new game post. On the other hand the tribesmen blamed her for the stricter supervision of poaching due to our presence. Furthermore a woman had recently been killed in Tanganyika by a tame lion and the D.C. now told me that the incident had been used to stimulate ill-feeling against Elsa. Also it was claimed that her friendship for us, by accustoming her to human beings, could make her a danger to strangers. He warned me that in the circumstances it might become necessary to remove Elsa from her home.

Four days later a rumour reached us that two tribesmen had been mauled by a lion fourteen miles from Elsa's camp. George left at once to investigate. He reached camp too late to pursue his inquiries. That evening Elsa and the cubs played happily round the tent; though they ate greedily they were in excellent condition, which was satisfactory as they had been left to themselves for seven days. As daylight broke George went to the Game Scouts' post; no one had heard of any tribesmen being mauled by a lion. So he sent the Scouts to the scene of the alleged accident and returned to camp.

In order to keep the lions near to the tents he gave them a

carcase which they dragged into a bush close by. They stayed there until the evening.

The day after George's hurried departure for the camp, I followed, bringing the truck as well as the Land-Rover. It was late when we arrived and the men were too tired to unload the truck and put the goats into it for the night. We therefore secured them in a thorn enclosure.

Although, as we had two cars, our arrival was noisy and Elsa must have heard us, she did not come to welcome me. This was the first time she had failed to do so.

After I had gone to bed I heard the cubs attacking the goats' boma. The sounds of breaking wood, growling lions and stampeding animals bleating, left no doubt as to what was happening. We rushed out but not before Elsa, Gopa and Little Elsa had each of them killed a goat. Jespah was holding one down with his paw which George was able to rescue unhurt.

It took us two hours to round up the bolting, panic-stricken survivors of the herd and secure them in the truck, while hyenas, attracted by the noise, circled round.

Elsa took her kill across the river. George who followed her saw a large crocodile making for Elsa and shot at it but missed it. He spent until 2 a.m. sitting close to Elsa to see if it would reappear, but it did not. The cubs were very much upset at finding themselves and their kills separated from Elsa by the river; after half an hour of anxious miaowing they joined their mother without having started to eat the goats they had killed.

In the afternoon, the Game Scouts returned; they had not got any confirmation of the rumour that tribesmen had been mauled by lions, but they had collected plenty of evidence to show that, influenced by poachers and political agitators, the tribesmen were becoming increasingly hostile to Elsa. We realised that her life was in danger and discussed what we should do.

We had spent six months in camp, much longer than we had originally planned, in order to protect Elsa and her cubs from poachers and by doing so had inevitably interfered with their natural life. If now we stayed on the cubs would become so tame that they would have little chance of adapting themselves in the future to the life of the bush.

Besides this, if we went on camping in the reserve we should only aggravate the antagonism of the tribesmen. Since we could not, in the circumstances, leave Elsa and the cubs alone, the only solution we could think of was to look for a new home for them and move them as soon as possible.

We had had great difficulty in finding a suitable place for Elsa's release; to find one for her and the cubs was likely to be still more difficult. We knew that by now, with their mother's help in teaching them to hunt and protecting them from natural foes they were capable of living the life of the bush; but where would they be safe, not only from wild animals but also from man, who now proved to be their most dangerous enemy?

Leaving me in charge of the camp, George returned next morning to Isiolo hoping to find a solution to this problem.

In the afternoon I walked with Nuru to the Whuffing Rock where we had spotted Elsa. She came down at once to greet us, but when I started to climb up the saddle to join the sleeping cubs, she prevented me from doing so by sitting squarely across my path, and only after we were on our way home did she call her children. Through my field-glasses I saw Jespah and Gopa climb down, but Little Elsa remained on top like a sentry.

When it was dark the family arrived in camp and after eating their dinner, Elsa and her sons played happily in the tent until they dozed off in a close embrace. I sketched them, while Little Elsa watched us from outside the tent. In the night a lion called and for the next three days he kept close to the camp. During this time Elsa stayed in the immediate vicinity. It was only after the lion had left the neighbourhood that she ventured to take the cubs to the Big Rock and then by tea-time she returned as though to ensure an early dinner undisturbed by the possible appearance of another lion.

I usually met the family on their way to camp and was often touched by Jespah's behaviour. When Elsa and I greeted each other he didn't want to be left out, but I think he knew that I was scared of his claws, for he would place himself with his rear towards me and keep absolutely still as though to assure me that

86

like this I would be quite safe from accidental scratches while I patted him. From then on he always adopted this attitude when he wanted to be stroked.

The 20th December was the cubs' first birthday. As a birthday treat I had a guinea fowl, which I cut up into four portions so that each should have a share. After gobbling these titbits Elsa hopped on to the Land-Rover while the cubs tore at some meat we had prepared for them.

As all the lions were happily occupied I called to Makedde to escort me for a walk. As soon as we set out Elsa jumped off the car and followed us; then Jespah, seeing his mother disappear, stopped his meal and ran after us, and we had not gone far before I saw Gopa and Little Elsa parallel to us chasing each other through the bush.

When we came to the place where the track comes nearest to the Big Rock, the lions sat down and rolled in the sand. I waited for a little while and watched the setting sun turn the rock to a bright red; then since Elsa looked settled, I walked back, expecting the family to spend the evening on the Rock. I was surprised when she followed me. She kept close so that I could help with the tsetse flies, and Jespah trotted next to us like a well-trained child. Gopa and Little Elsa took their time; they scampered about a long way behind us and we often had to stop to wait for them.

Elsa seemed to have come along just to join me in my walk; this was the first time she had done so since the cubs were born. I thought it a charming way of celebrating their birthday.

When we arrived in camp Elsa flung herself on the ground inside my tent and was joined by her sons who nuzzled and embraced their mother with their paws. I sketched them until Elsa retired to the roof of the Land-Rover and the cubs started to eat their dinner. When I was sure that the cubs would not observe me I went over to Elsa and stroked her and she responded very affectionately. I wanted to thank her for having shared her children with us during their first year, and having shared her anxieties during the period which is so full of dangers for any young animals. But, after some time, as though to remind me that in spite of our friendship we belonged to two different worlds, a lion suddenly started roaring and after listening intently Elsa left.

Next morning we found the spoor of a lioness upstream, but no trace of Elsa. She did not turn up that day or during the following night. On the second night we heard two lions roaring and understood why she had not come to camp. I was, therefore, astonished to see her next morning about 9 a.m. on the Whuffing Rock, roaring as hard as she could. I called to her but she paid no attention and went on roaring for an hour. To whom was she calling at this unusual time of day?

She brought her cubs in for dinner that night but when a lion started roaring she left at once, crossing the river.

Elsa and the cubs spent the night of 23rd December in camp and after breakfast when I strolled along the road to read in the sand the report on last night's visitors, she and the cubs followed me. I called to Makedde and we all walked along together for about two miles.

We went on until we came to a rain pool where the lions had a drink. By now the sun was getting hot and it would not have surprised me had Elsa decided to spend the day in this place, but good-naturedly she turned back when we did and trotted slowly home with us.

I could not help feeling as though we were all taking our Sunday family walk. Though in fact this was the morning of Christmas Eve, and Elsa could have no knowledge of special days, by a strange coincidence she had chosen a day I felt the need to commemorate by coming for a walk with me and bringing her family with her.

Elsa and the cubs were feeling the increasing heat very much and often stopped under the shade of a tree to rest, yet when we came near the Big Rock they suddenly rushed at full speed through the bush and in a few leaps reached the top, where they settled among the boulders. I scrambled after them as best I could, but Elsa made it quite plain that I should now leave them alone. She always knew exactly how much she felt it was fitting for her to give to each of her two worlds, so I confined myself to taking some photographs of her guarding her cubs.

George arrived about tea-time with a suitcase full of mail. While we strolled about picking flowers for Christmas decorations, he told me of the inquiries he had made about finding a new home for Elsa and the cubs. He thought that the Lake Rudolph area would be the place in which the lions would be safest from human interference. He had obtained permission from the authorities to take them there if the need arose, and was soon going to reconnoitre the region to find a suitable spot.

This part of Kenya is very grim and conditions are tough there, so I felt depressed at the prospect. To make matters worse Elsa chose this moment to join us on our way home; behind her the cubs were playing happily along the road, and I could not bear to visualise them roaming on the wind-swept, lava-strewn desert which surrounds the lake.

When we reached camp we gave the family their supper which kept them occupied while I arranged the table for our Christmas dinner. I decorated it with flowers and tinsel ornaments and put the little silver Christmas tree I had kept from last year in the middle and a still smaller one which had just arrived from London in front of it. Then I brought out the presents for George and the boys.

Jespah watched my preparations very carefully and the moment I turned my back to get the candles he rushed up and seized a parcel which contained a shirt for George, and bounced off with it into a thicket. Gopa joined him immediately and the two of them had a wonderful time with the shirt. When at last we rescued it it was in no state to give to George.

By now it was nearly dark and I started to light the candles. That was all Jespah needed to make him decide to come and help me. I only just managed to prevent him from pulling the table-cloth, with the decorations and burning candles, on top of himself. It needed a lot of coaxing to make him keep away so that I could light the rest of the candles.

When all was ready he came up, tilted his head, looked at the glittering Christmas trees and then sat down and watched the candles burn lower and lower. As each flame went out I felt as though another happy day of our life in the camp had passed. When all the lights had gone out the darkness seemed intense and as though it were a symbol of the darkness of our future. A few yards away Elsa and her cubs rested peacefully in the grass, hardly visible in the fading light.

Afterwards George and I read our mail. It took us many hours to do so, during which our imaginations travelled across the world and brought us close to all the people who were wishing Elsa and her family and us happiness.

Mercifully it was one of the last envelopes I opened which contained an order for the removal of Elsa and her cubs from the reserve.

Elsa's Camp, 24th December, 1960

Forever Free

JOY ADAMSON

Elsa has died, leaving her three cubs, Jespah, Gopa and Little Elsa at just over a year old and incapable of fending for themselves. A second blow was struck when the cubs were ordered out of Kenya.

This was the beginning of a nightmarish ordeal for the Adamsons. The cubs were to be moved over 600 miles to the Serengeti in Tanganyika, but they could not be trapped. They began to raid the local villages in search of food. Night after night, they broke through thorn enclosures and carried off goats and fowl. The villagers lived in fear for their lives and the Adamsons for the lives of the cubs.

But at last the move was accomplished. The three cubs were loosed into the wild – forever free.

Joy Adamson's famous books about Elsa, *Born Free*, *Living Free* and *Forever Free* have inspired two of the most popular animal films of all time. *Born Free* and *Living Free* are also Armada Lions.

By the Sandhills of Yamboorah

REGINALD OTTLEY

Reginald Ottley was fifteen when he started to work as a wood-and-water joey on a cattle station in Australia. He then became cattle-drover, horse-breaker, and wanderer across the vast outback.

In *By the Sandhills of Yamboorah* he describes with perception and warmth the life of a boy on a cattle station and the land he knows so well.

This book won the New York Herald Tribune Children's Spring Book Festival Prize in 1966 and was runner-up in Australia for the Award for Best Children's Book of 1965.

'Conveys powerfully the feel of Australia and the feeling of adolescence. This is a notable addition to Australian children's literature.'   *The Times Literary Supplement*

'Its value lies in its accurate representation. . .of the life of a boy isolated in an entirely adult society.'
                                            Australian Book Review

Marguerite Henry

MISTY OF CHINCOTEAGUE
SEA STAR, ORPHAN OF CHINCOTEAGUE
STORMY, MISTY'S FOAL

Just off the coast of Virginia lie the islands of Chincoteague
and Assateague. On Assateague, ponies run wild all the
year except on Pony Penning Day, when the men from
Chincoteague come over to round up the herd. The wild
and beautiful Phantom had always escaped them, but young
Paul Beebe and his sister Maureen are determined to tame
her. They miraculously succeed in bringing Phantom and
her colt Misty back to Chincoteague.

In *Sea Star* Misty has been sold and Paul and Maureen
are heart-broken until they find a new-born foal on the
beach of Assateague. They call the colt Sea Star and take
him home to Chincoteague, but Sea Star refuses to eat
and it seems that he won't survive for long . . .

In *Stormy* disaster strikes the islands of Assateague and
Chincoteague as the sea swallows up the land and its
inhabitants in a tidal storm. The Beebes have to evacuate
and leave behind Misty who is about to foal.

King of the Wind by Marguerite Henry is also a Lion.
Perfect for eight-year-olds and upwards.

Panther

RODERICK HAIG-BROWN

Ki-yu's father had been the meanest panther on Vancouver Island. Ki-yu grew up to be just as mean and even more cunning. Every living thing became his enemy – man especially.

The seasons passed in killing, feeding, and roaming, sometimes with a mate, sometimes alone. With his brute strength Ki-yu brought down deer, wolves, and even a bear. Then out of daring and disdain he came down from the mountains to attack the farm animals. And so he became the hunted as well as the hunter.

David Milton was the best panther hunter on the island. For two years he pursued Ki-yu relentlessly, tracking him with all his skill and knowledge, only to lose him time and again.

But both the panther and the man knew that in the end only one of them could survive. . .